IF
THE
WORLD
ONLY
KNEW

WHAT SIXTY-SIX YOUNG AUTHORS BELIEVE

PUBLISHED MAY 2015 BY 826 VALENCIA
COPYRIGHT © 2015 BY 826 VALENCIA
ALL RIGHTS RESERVED BY 826 VALENCIA AND THE AUTHORS
ISBN 978-1-934750-59-9

PROGRAM MANAGER AND EDITOR
Molly Parent

PROGRAM DIRECTOR
Christina V. Perry

EDITORIAL ASSISTANTS
Pablo Baeza and Desta Lissanu

EDITORIAL BOARD
Alejandra Galvan, Christopher Archilla, Darryl Forman, Elia Gonzalez, Elise Wise, Emajae Hackett, Eve Lebwohl, Halley Roberts, Henry Bradley, Jessica Ramirez, Kevin Wofsy, Lindsey Bourne, Mari Amend, Naveen Agrawal, Riley Clark, Ryan Haas, Sian Laing, Shauna Bogetz, Tehan Carey, Terri Cohn, William Poole, and Yancy Castro

DESIGN DIRECTOR
María Inés Montes

PRODUCTION COORDINATOR
Amy Popovich

BOOK DESIGNER
Lauren Mulkey

COPY EDITOR
Will Georgantas

Printed in Canada by Prolific Graphics.

IF THE WORLD ONLY KNEW

WHAT SIXTY-SIX YOUNG AUTHORS BELIEVE

Essays by ninth graders at Mission High School
With a foreword by Glynn Washington, host of Snap Judgment

SMALL ACTS OF BEAUTY
Stories of One Person vs. the World

IT'S OURS
Stories of Community

THE COMPASS WITHIN
Stories of Change

FOREWORD

BY GLYNN WASHINGTON

When I was young, I knew the end of the world was nigh.

My parents, my pastor, my community, and I lived in the Last Days awaiting the cataclysmic tribulation foretold in our books. Every night, we thanked God for moving us twenty-four hours closer to the End of Days. Every morning I woke up grateful that our Apostle, Herbert W. Armstrong, understood the hidden signs.

The Apostle promised me that I would never have a wife, never have a child, and never grow old because we were leaving all that behind. Soon, very soon, I would be whisked into the sky with other true believers to meet my Creator, while the world burned in torment.

I felt sad for the unbelievers, but they lived in sin.

One day in middle school, my teacher asked everyone to imagine themselves in ten years, and write down what we saw. I took the assignment seriously, and sketched out a vision of myself floating amongst the clouds, looking down at the confusion and horror of my neighbors. I wrote describing how former schoolmates would turn their faces toward the sun and see me, glowing with divine power. They would marvel, even as I shook my head in pity at their plight.

I finished the account, and read it to myself. I turned the paper upside down, and read it that way. I held it in my hands, and read it once more. Seeing the scene written down gave it an odd weight, like wearing someone else's socks or describing someone else's dream. I saw someone else's words, scribbled in my handwriting.

I tried again, with a new sheet of paper. I thought of my friend Jason, who had brought a bongo drum back from his trip to the Bahamas. I imagined a future where I learned to beat Jason's drum. I played his drum for the president, and the president danced. I played for the queen and my uncles, and the girls at the lake, and the farmers in the fields, and the boys washing cars, and the men in the office, and the ladies at the store, and they all danced together, following me and Jason's drum as we banged down the street.

I laughed out loud while writing of drum-dancing dogs and two-stepping trees. I finished by describing a flock of green-and-gold parrots beating their wings in rhythm as they flew into an ocean of song.

Finally, I put down my pencil. I read each of my two supposed futures. Both felt absurd. But one I believed.

So I gave my teacher the paper about the drum and tossed the other into the trash.

And that night, for the first time ever in my young life, I went to bed uncertain.

I have remained uncertain ever since.

The collection of essays you are reading are about beliefs examined up close. Measured. Weighted. Considered. In a lot of ways, the essays are also about uncertainty. These young heroes routinely walk to the edge of reality's plank and jump off without a safety net. They make mistakes. They act with insufficient information. They hurt. They fail. They do all the things the rest of us do and they do it when it matters most.

Then they try again.

We get to watch these young authors discover the Quantum Nature of Belief, which goes like this: observation alters belief.

As they write what they believe, they first examine what they believe. And as they examine what they believe, they change what they believe.

(When you change what you believe, you change who you are.)

This is what we see happening in these pages—people changing who they are. The best part of watching them grow on the page is that we feel permission to grow with them.

In so many ways, this book is a mirror. In reading about these young people's lives, I found myself remembering my own struggle. Often, I wanted to whisper in their ear, "Monsters lurk that way! Turn back now!" But just as I didn't have an omniscient adviser alerting me to life's pitfalls, these authors don't either.

It's probably for the best. As a young person, I wouldn't have appreciated some overstuffed know-it-all shouting instructions.

But if someone did show up, I would hope they brought a drum.

* * *

Before creating the storytelling radio show Snap Judgment, *Glynn Washington worked as an educator, a diplomat, a community activist, an actor, a political strategist, fist-shaker, mountain-hollerer, and foot-stomper. Glynn has composed music for the Kunst Stoff dance performance in San Francisco, joined a band in Indonesia, written several screenplays, painted a daring series of self-portraits, and knows for a fact that these young people can accomplish anything.*

INTRODUCTION

BY CHRISTOPHER ARCHILLA, HENRY BRADLEY, YANCY
AME CASTRO, RILEY CLARK, ALEJANDRA GALVAN, ELIA
GONZALEZ, AND SIAN LAING

Because we're only freshmen in high school, some people might think we don't have many life experiences. But at this critical moment in our lives—in which we've just entered high school, are making transitions, and are growing older and taller—it's particularly important to us to define ourselves. Sometimes it feels like it's us against the world.

Our English teacher, Mr. Anders, gave us the opportunity to work on this project and publish a book with the help of writing tutors from 826 Valencia. When we first heard about the project, we didn't know what to expect. Some of us thought we would get to write anything we wanted—fiction, even. Then Mr. Anders gave us our prompt: write about something you believe, and why. We asked, Do we have to write about ourselves? Do our stories have to be true? The thought of writing stories about ourselves made us apprehensive. Also, in the beginning, not many of us were thrilled with the idea of working with tutors. The thought of working on an essay for a whole month sounded daunting and tedious. In addition to this, many students were afraid of sharing their personal stories, interacting with strangers, and having an adult looking over their shoulder for the entire process.

We didn't know where to start. We had to choose a belief. This wasn't the hard part, though—the hard part was explaining why we believed it. We were encouraged to come up with stories that explained our beliefs. Piecing the stories together was like trying to sew together Frankenstein's body. We had to force our brains to think about our experiences and how to express them. Once we jumped into writing, though, our ideas slowly came together and the big picture came into view. We surprised ourselves with our ability to not only choose a belief, but to craft a narrative that showed our ideas. Through this process, we all began to bond with our tutors and realize that the task of writing an essay about our beliefs was not as difficult as we thought.

Many of us were completely surprised by how much we benefited from the few weeks with our tutors. Through the amazing process and careful guidance, a special trust developed between us and our tutors that helped us find things we wouldn't have discovered on our own. We also wrote more, because the tutors were people we got along with, and they were interested in our lives. That's something we don't always feel when we're writing an essay, so we pushed ourselves extra hard. When we first started, we felt like we would have so much time to finish, but at the end of each day, it always felt like there was so much more to write. It seemed like we were never done with the work of writing—except then, suddenly, we were. Looking back, the process is like a blur.

During the editorial stage, we noticed that many of the essays collected here have themes of struggle. Many of us think that teenagers shouldn't be struggling with the same things adults are struggling with. Our stories aren't always happy, but they're also not always sad. Reading the work of our peers, we realized that we all have different roads we're traveling on, and each road has both happiness and struggle. These feelings will always be combined, and they'll always both be there. Those paths will cross, and we'll connect at that intersection, and then we'll go our own ways again.

In writing this book, we've been wondering how the world will receive it. We're guessing that the world will be surprised to hear how we think and what we think about. We hope that one thing we're teaching the world is that being an adult doesn't mean you can't express yourself like a teenager. We also want people to see that we are sharing authentic beliefs that are shared by adults, but we are a new generation with new struggles, with unique thoughts that are all ours. Every year we learn something new, and it helps our beliefs adapt as we grow up and become adults ourselves. We are teaching the world about expression through the openness in our writing.

Our beliefs started as simple ideas on pieces of paper. But through the writing process, they became a much deeper conviction. The process of writing these essays helped us to define our beliefs, and to get deeper into them. What we learned was that the process embodied the theme. The act of writing was like the act of believing. We had to commit to accomplishing the task and to trust in ourselves.

Not everyone has the same perspective. Each mind is its own world. We all have different beliefs, but we can connect over the ones we share. This is why we wrote this book. It's because we have to stand up for what we believe, and show the world that we can climb even higher.

I NEED TO THANK YOU FOR THAT

STORIES OF ROLE MODELS

Elia Gonzalez was born in 1999 in El Salvador. Six years ago she arrived in San Francisco and immediately started learning English. Now she is a freshman at Mission High School and loves to eat fruit salad and play with her dog, Prince.

WORDS FROM A WISE MAN

BY ELIA GONZALEZ

My uncle Jorge wasn't the type of guy to be nice. He gave you love his way: the gangster way. He grew up being in a gang. With his friends, he was hard. He never showed any feelings around them, and no love. He would say that he didn't care about life, about anybody. But he was a whole different person when he was with me versus when he was with his friends.

With me, he was caring and loving. He used to show me how much he cared for our family by giving us love and being there for us unconditionally. But people would look at him the wrong way. You could see their eyes narrow as they looked at him, sizing him up, but they just didn't know what an amazing man he was. The streets couldn't see him being "soft," but he was the first love of my life. He raised me tough like a boy, but with love so that my heart would be soft. He was smart and wise.

My uncle Jorge has been my father figure my whole life. I am who I am because of him. He was serious most of the time, but when he was funny, he could make you cry with laughter. He taught me all my values: how to be nice, how to keep on going, and how to try to understand life even when it seems impossible. Most of all, he taught me how to be kind to people no matter what. He said, "Be kind to people; you never know when you will need them. And you can maybe, just maybe, change the world to a better place. To a better tomorrow." To be honest, when he initially said it, I didn't believe him. It sounded stupid at first.

He tried his best to show me what being kind is and what it looks like. I know it was hard for him. He was raised being a "G," and "kind" wasn't in his vocabulary when he was growing up. But he showed me how being kind can put a smile on people's faces, or make their day. I asked him once, "Is being kind a value?" And he said, "No, *mija*, being kind comes from your heart. It comes from you."

Before he taught me this, I had never been kind to people. I used to believe that if you had a hard heart, it was better because people wouldn't step on you. So it was hard to be kind to others. I used to be really selfish. I would never think of others; everything had to do with me only. Someone would ask me for help or advice, but I would just turn my back on them. When my friend Madeline would come up to me and ask me what she should do about a problem, I would just say, "I don't know," and change the subject. Why? Because if I helped her I wouldn't get anything in return.

But then, one time, one of my friends was going through some stuff. I could tell because she was depressed, and you could see it written all over her face. At first, I didn't know how to help. It wasn't something I thought I could help with. I didn't want to get into her family problems. But this time, I needed to. She was like a sister to me, and I needed to do something for her. I couldn't give her my back. I thought it was going to be difficult, but I started with something as simple as a smile, and I know she felt supported by me. Later on, I heard she did the same thing with someone else. She was there for her friend, like I had been for her. This taught me that if you're kind to someone, that person will probably be kind to someone else who is struggling with something. I thought back to what my uncle said about how kindness

ELIA GONZALEZ

"I asked him once, 'Is being kind a value?' And he said, 'No *mija*, being kind comes from your heart. It comes from you."

can change the world. I realized I had changed the world that day, even if only in a small way.

One act of kindness that I appreciated was when my uncle gave my sister some advice. My sister is three years older than me. She was sixteen at the time. They weren't close, though, and didn't really talk because he thought she was childish for her age. But I told him she was going through some problems with her boyfriend. My uncle told me he was going to be there for her and talk to her.

He was locked up at the time, which meant we had to go down to the jail to see him. When we got there, a lot of people were waiting to see their loved ones. We went at night, and the place was unwelcoming. The jail was a cinder block, dark and chilly, and all you could hear were people's footsteps and the voices of the police officers saying, "Go left," or "Go up the steps." Even though they hadn't been close, when my sister needed some guidance in her life, my uncle was there. He made sure she could count on someone if she was going through a hard time in her life. Things didn't go the way he wanted because she didn't end up taking his advice, but he tried and my sister knew he loved her. Kindness doesn't always work the way you want or expect, but she could keep that memory of our visit in her mind. And sooner or later she would take his advice into consideration.

I don't believe in many things. I mean, what's the point? Isn't the world messed up anyway? I mean, why believe in something if it's not going to change people? And to change the world, we need to change people first. But I was beginning to see that by being kind, I could make people believe in kindness, and in that way, I could change the world.

I believe in God, but not everyone does. Some people don't want to believe in religion. Why? Because there are so many rules. But why not believe in something without rules? In something you can do at any time and everywhere? Being kind to someone is not hard! You don't need money to be kind. You can give a stranger a smile, and that can make that person's day. The world has enough hate already; a little bit of kindness wouldn't be too much to ask for. You can do someone a big favor by telling them they're beautiful or by giving them a hand when they need it. It will come back to you. Just like they say, "What goes around, comes around."

People are unkind because we live in a society with racism, bullying, crime, and hate. Another reason why people are unkind is because they cannot deal with their own problems, and therefore can't deal with someone else's problems. I know for me, if I'm going through some stuff, I don't want to help others because I want to be helped instead. But people should be kind, and I always try to be kind, because it makes us better people and opens more doors in our lives. I believe that kindness can be the key to a better world.

If everyone believed in this, then the world would be a better place. It would be calmer. People would be nicer to each other. There wouldn't be wars, teenagers killing each other, or families destroyed. With more kindness, there wouldn't be so much hate around the world. Can kindness change the world? I don't know for sure, but I think so, and like my uncle said, it's worth a try.

I remember when my uncle started being kind to people. It felt weird because he wasn't that type of guy. The community didn't know him like that. He spent his whole life being locked up. And it hurt because that was time we lost. He wasn't bad; he just made bad decisions. But he also made me who I am, and I am proud of it. He taught me lots of things, like how to be respectful, caring, helpful, and kind to others. He was a great man. God let me borrow him for some years, and I am really thankful for that. I know that before he died, he wanted me to help change the world by being kind. Now I'm doing it in his memory.

Zoe Olson was born in Seattle, Washington, but has spent the last ten years in San Francisco. Zoe is fourteen years old. She loves pesto pizza. Despite her fear of heights, Zoe would like to be able to fly.

LESSONS IN LITERATURE

BY ZOE OLSON

"The way I see it, every life is a pile of good things and bad things. The good things don't always soften the bad things, but vice versa: the bad things don't necessarily spoil the good things and make them unimportant."

— The Doctor

In the show *Doctor Who*, Amy and the Doctor travel back in time to meet Vincent Van Gogh to show him the brighter side of life before he kills himself months later. When Amy, who has fallen in love with him, laments to the Doctor that they haven't made a difference in Van Gogh's life, the Doctor shares his lesson about how there are always good things that come with the bad. Later, when Amy steps forward on the cold white museum tiles to study a painting by the artist, she sees a bouquet of sunflowers, her favorite flower, and a dedication in her name.

The Doctor showed me how the little things that restore our faith in the world are the most important. It has always been lessons like these, which books, movies, and TV have taught me, that stick with me as the most important lessons in my life. I believe that good stories have the power to change people.

Books like the Harry Potter series teach readers that there is always hope, that love beats hate, and that you make your own family. When you read a story that works its way into your heart and settles down to live there, it stays with you forever. As a teenager who hasn't had any enormous life-shaping experiences, the lessons that books teach us are really the only ones I've learned for myself.

Sometimes it's difficult to find a story that teaches us something important. Stereotypical teen stories all seem to have the same storyline, like products on a factory line. It goes: in a dystopian future, a girl or boy is somehow different and destined to lead a group of outcasts in a rebellion against the oppressive government. On the way there will be lots of drama around the love interest or love triangle. There will also probably be some form of powers. And lots of people will die. Sometimes you find a story that defies the stereotypes, or also has different lessons.

Once in a while you find a book, film, or TV show that tells an entirely different story. There are many that value family and friends just as much as romance. Marvel movies, *The Lord of the Rings*, Harry Potter, and more teach us that finding friends and family who accept your differences is just as important. Roald Dahl books, Miyazaki movies, *Alice in Wonderland,* and *The Chronicles of Narnia* tell us to keep our imaginations alive and breathing, and to never forget our childhood. *The Tiger Rising*, *Finding Neverland*, *The Secret Garden*, the Young Sherlock Holmes series, and *Up* all tell us there is life after death. Artemis Fowl shows us that people change. Doctor Who and Sherlock say that our lives and the people in them are much more than they appear. Even if you don't like to read, you know that fiction can influence millions of people. Even if you haven't read the books or watched the movies, you know who Harry Potter is. Fiction is powerful.

People who read are more likely to empathize with others. When we read, we learn what it's like in another person's head without really seeing what they actually look like—we can't judge them because we have never actually seen them. We get to know a person, their feelings, and their perspective from the inside out. It's this power that changes the way a person sees other people and the world, and teaches us lessons that help us see it as a better place.

Christopher Martinez lives in San Francisco and is fourteen years old. After he graduates from Mission High School he hopes to go to the University of Oregon, the University of Alabama, Texas A&M, or Ohio State to play football. He plays left tackle.

FOOTBALL IS MY WAY OUT

BY CHRISTOPHER MARTINEZ

"I make my players practice real hard because if a player is a quitter, I want him to quit in practice, not in a game."

— Bear Bryant

"It's all down to this play for the Galileo Lions to take the Turkey Bowl Championship again," says the announcer. Juan Martinez, playing left tackle, has to buck out the defensive end. They are running a thirty-three blast. They snap the ball, and Juan Martinez knocks down the defensive end. He starts running upfield like a jaguar to block for his halfback. "Galileo is at the twenty, fifteen, ten, five, TOUCHDOWN! GALILEO TAKES IT ALL FOR THE SECOND YEAR!"

Everyone starts jumping and cheering from the sidelines and the stands; they name Juan Martinez the MVP and Best Offensive Lineman of the Year. The coach tells him that he is the best offensive lineman he's seen and that he has so much heart and pride for the game, for football itself. He gets calls from Colorado State, UCLA, Alabama, USC, and the University of Oregon, but he can't attend any of the colleges because he doesn't have documents to show he was born in the United States.

Before all of this happened, Juan lived in Mexico. He believed in work and money because he didn't have an education. He didn't have any other beliefs until he moved to the United States. He graduated from James Lick Middle School in San Francisco. Then he went to Galileo High School. He first started playing soccer, then found interest in football, but the football coach said he wouldn't survive on the team. Then he made the coach feel dumb about making that decision. Juan became the best left tackle they ever had. They named him MVP twice and Best Offensive Lineman twice.

Juan Martinez is my dad, and he knew that football was a way out. Coming from a culture where gangs and poverty were the only thing he knew, he found football as something that would set him free. Some of my uncles were out in the streets serving the block and gangbanging. My dad observed what they were doing, but knew that if he were to do the same thing, he wouldn't be setting the right example for all of us. That's why he chose football instead of serving on the block like some of my uncles did. He told me when I first started playing football that this isn't just a sport. It's a way out of the world we're living in.

Michael Oher was an African American who lived on the rough side of Memphis, Tennessee, without a way out. Then he started playing football in high school at Briarcrest Christian High School. He didn't know how to play, but he kept learning, and soon he got noticed when he started playing and doing great at left tackle. He agreed to go to Mississippi for college. He did well in school and got drafted from Mississippi. He then attended the NFL and ran 5.32 seconds in his forty-yard dash, 4.6 seconds in his twenty-yard shuttle run, and 7.59 seconds in the three-cone drill, and jumped 30.5 inches for his vertical jump and 103 inches in his broad jump. Oher's story connects to my belief because even though Michael

Oher was a rookie just starting off playing football, he made it to the big leagues. He had heart for playing the game because it was a way out for him, a way to escape from where he was raised. Football gave him a caring family who wanted the best for him, took him in. From there he made it to a place where only a small percentage of people make it. He knew football was a way out for him.

Football does transform people in different ways, just like it transformed Aldon Smith, who messed up but eventually got all of his stuff together. Aldon Smith got arrested for a DUI in the beginning of the 2014 season with the 49ers. He then got arrested for screaming "Bomb!" in an airport, which was stupid. The NFL suspended him for nine games, but after those nine games he changed. He came back to the game a different person. He told the media that he was going to be a better person, and he was. He avoided problems with the law. When he started practicing he was practicing harder; he came back after his suspension and got 4.5 sacks in the game. After that he was averaging 2.0 sacks a game. Because he avoided getting into trouble, he is settling a contract extension with the 49ers. Aldon Smith knew that if he messed up in the 2015 season, he would be cut off the team. That's why he puts more effort into his work instead of slacking off, being benched, and not being able to play because of foolish decisions. When he's off the field, he has to think about his decisions and the consequences.

I remember when it was a sunny day in San Francisco and the Daly City Stars were playing the Hayward Earthquakes. I was on the offensive line and I was blocking someone bigger than me. He was six four, 390 pounds, and he kept pushing me around like a rag doll. During halftime my dad yanked me to the side to talk to me.

"Get it together! Why is he pushing you around, huh? Pick your head up and block him! Just because he's bigger than you doesn't give him an advantage over you. Put your anger and weight on him. Show him just because he's big doesn't mean he'll win. Show him how much heart you have to be able to block someone that big!"

It was third and two, and the play was going to my side. "Hut!" The ball was snapped. I snatched his pads and started pushing him. I threw him on the floor, but he got up quick and tried to hit our running back. So I turned around and hit him. He fell and he was lying on the floor holding his ribs. We scored and secured the game. I went over and helped him up to show sportsmanship. Afterward he told me I had a lot of heart for taking those hits and still managing to get up and play every down of the game, no matter how messed up I looked. Then he told me to keep going at it, no matter how big your opponent is. Even though he was bigger than me and will have a better chance at getting a scholarship than I will, I know if I keep hustling I'll have the same chance as he will, and that will be my way out.

Without this belief my life would honestly be crap. Before all this football happened I had bad grades. I didn't have qualifying grades for any type of sport in school, so I had to play in outside leagues because they didn't check my grades. I was smoking weed before I found my belief. I got into deep trouble with weed and I decided to change, so I stopped and started running and conditioning for football. Once I started playing football I told myself to hustle through every practice, no matter how tired I would get. Even if I felt like throwing up I'd keep hustling through it. If I threw up, I threw up, but I had to keep practicing and not throw in the towel. I have to keep going, strive, and succeed through it, because at the end everything I work for is going to pay off.

I am where I want to be, football-wise. Grade-wise, I have yet to improve, but I know that I can, and I have to if I want to attend the attend the University of Oregon. I have talked to other coaches at different schools, mostly private schools, to see if they could try to find a way for Oregon to come scout me so I have a better chance at achieving my dream. The coaches told me to change my ways in school and stop slacking off, not doing work, and not passing my classes. I'm doing it slowly. I've got a long way to go, but I know I can pull through and make it. Both my cousins are playing because they know being a Pacific Islander is like having an advantage in football. All three of us play so we'll have a way out of where we came from. Where we're from, there are just gangs and poverty for us. That's why I turned my life around. I don't want to see my mom and dad suffering to pay for my college; I'd rather get to college on a scholarship and show them that I can make something out of my life instead of living in gangs and poverty.

Football changed how I see and live life. We all play for a reason; some play for money and fame, I play for a way out of where I am from. All my cousins play this sport because they want to show people that they made something of themselves. We all play for the love of the game and we want to be someone people look up to. Life every day is a struggle for us, and that's why we found football; it's a way out of where we come from. With football, it seems like life is easier for us in a way. My aunt always tells me this quote when I get out of church: *"La fa'afualoaina pea ae le atua soifua."* May God continue to lengthen your days. I hope he does, so I can keep living life and playing football.

Theresa Rodriguez was born in San Francisco fifteen years ago. Her parents were born in El Salvador. She has three sisters and a brother, so it's a good thing she likes to cook. A superpower she would love to have is telepathy. After she graduates from high school, she wants to go to college, and after college, she hopes to go to medical school.

PUTTING MY LIFE IN ORDER

BY THERESA RODRIGUEZ

Everyone needs beliefs to keep their life in order. But one day in the spring when I was in eighth grade, my life fell out of order.

I was about to enter James Lick Middle School when I saw my friend Ariel. I went to where she was standing. Everyone was going up the steps into school before the bell rang. She took me aside and led me down the steps. *Where are we going?* I wondered.

At the bottom of the steps she whispered, " I didn't finish my math presentation. I don't want to get in trouble. Did you finish yours?"

"Yes," I replied cautiously. "Why?"

"Because I don't want to go to school," she said.

"What if we get caught?" I asked.

"We won't," she said. "Come on, let's go."

She pulled my arm. I hesitated. I had finished my presentation on linear equations, but I was very shy and I didn't like the math teacher, Ms. Houston. She was strict, always grouchy, and she was scary. I wasn't looking forward to giving my presentation, even though I was a straight-A student.

I looked at Ariel. "Where would we go?" I asked.

The bell was about to ring. I had to decide quickly. Other kids were swarming past us into the school. *What should I do?* I wondered. My mom would kill me if I skipped school.

"Hurry up. It's just one day," Ariel urged. "We won't get caught. Let's go to the pier and hang out."

The bell rang. I panicked and said yes. Before I knew what was happening, we were running to catch the bus for the pier. On the bus, I immediately started thinking over my decision. Here I was, a straight-A student. I had never done anything like this before. What would happen if we got caught? The school would call our parents. We might get suspended. We would have to make up our schoolwork.

Losing my mom's trust would be worse than making up schoolwork.

Even worse than doing my presentation for scary Ms. Houston would be getting the silent treatment from my mom. For a whole day, no matter how much I would beg my mom to talk to me, she would be silent. She wouldn't answer my questions. She would just ignore me. That would make me feel sad, guilty, and ashamed of myself. My mom's silent treatment was powerful. I was already feeling it just sitting on the bus with Ariel.

"We shouldn't be doing this," I said. "We should go back."

"Stop worrying," she laughed. "We won't get in trouble. One time won't hurt."

Ariel was a lot braver than me. She was a good friend, but she tried stuff that I would never do. She smoked and drank. She skipped school all the time and she got bad grades. She was really funny, though. And she could be nice. If I didn't have money in the cafeteria at lunchtime, she would share her money or her lunch. I felt like I could tell her anything. I could trust her with my deepest secrets.

At the pier we went to McDonald's. While I was enjoying my smoothie, I started to forget my guilt. I felt free and like something

THERESA RODRIGUEZ

had lifted off my chest. I felt relieved that I didn't have to do my presentation for scary Ms. Houston.

"Hey," I said to Ariel. "You were right. This is actually kind of fun."

"What did I tell you?" she laughed. "You never listen."

I started to wonder why being a good girl was so important to me. Here I was with my friend Ariel, having the best time and not worrying about anything. The way Ariel talked reminded me a little of my older cousin Karla.

Karla may not be as immature as Ariel, but she is irresponsible, especially when it comes to money. Karla has a job but she always wastes her money on unnecessary things. When Karla runs out of money she comes to my family, asking if she can borrow some from us. My mom is always telling me not to follow in Karla's footsteps. I wondered what my mom would think of if she could see me now sitting in McDonald's with Ariel laughing and talking instead of going to school.

"Hey, let's go chill out in the park," said Ariel as we finished our smoothies.

"No way," I said, feeling my old fearful self returning. "My sister works by there, and if she sees me she is going to kill me. For sure she'll tell my mom," I said.

"We'll have fun! Nobody even passes by Garfield Park," she said.

On the bus I was biting my nails for fear of getting caught. I was giving in to Ariel too easily, I thought. I was almost having too much fun. What if I got used to skipping school? My grades would slip. I would probably hang out with Ariel's friends, the wrong crowd. I might even start drinking and smoking. How hard would it be to regain my family's trust if I did that?

Looking out the window I saw some drunks drinking, and it reminded me of my cousin Roger. Roger is in his early thirties, but he has been drinking since he was a teen. His drinking has led to jail time and getting in trouble with the law. My whole family is always disappointed in him. We want to help him with his addiction but he's in denial. His life is still about partying.

I looked over at Ariel. She was listening to her music and bored, killing time. There was something about how she looked. I knew I didn't want to end up like that. At the park it was fun swinging on the swings and acting like little kids. But then there was nothing to do but be scared of someone seeing us before three o'clock when school ended.

* * *

"How was school today?" my mom asked when I walked into the house.

My hands started to sweat. My stomach twisted with fear. I tried not to act too nervous because my mom might notice and ask if something was wrong.

"Fine. Nothing special," I said. "I'm tired, I think I'll go take a nap."

I hurried to my room. Right away I felt guilty. When my mom called me for dinner, I took my seat at the table and stared at my food. I wanted to hide under a rock.

"Are you sure there's nothing wrong?" my mom asked.

I couldn't say I was tired because I had just taken a nap. I didn't say anything, I just ate my food quickly. Then I went back to my room. I tried to distract myself by watching some dumb YouTube videos on my phone. But when it was time to sleep, the guilt came back big-time. I didn't get the silent treatment from my mom because she didn't find out. But guilt and remorse haunted me all night and for days afterward.

I never skipped school again. As time passed I realized that it wasn't only about being a good daughter. What was the point of being a good daughter if your only motivation for being that way is your fear of being punished with the silent treatment? It was about my future. I like order in my life. One thing I learned from skipping school was that days filled with nothing but killing time made me nervous and guilty. I like to live according to a plan that I create. I like the feeling of accomplishment and the feeling of being a role model in my family. Family is one of my biggest values in life. I would have lost my mom's trust that day if she had found out that I skipped school. But I got lucky.

In middle school I believed in being a good, obedient daughter. Now that I'm in high school, I believe that trouble is a way to learn from your mistakes. When I was being a good, obedient daughter, I never thought of things like this. I just did what I was told, because I thought I had to, and if I didn't, I would be punished. Now that I'm older and have seen for myself what it's like to take chances and risk getting in trouble, I realize that my desire for an orderly life, good grades, and a plan for the future comes from a healthy belief that's deep inside me. It might sound strange, but I'm grateful that I skipped school that day. It strengthened my trust and belief in myself and my ability to plan my future.

Anthony Jones was born and raised in San Francisco. He is fourteen years old. He likes to play soccer and video games, and also enjoys playing the trumpet. Pizza is his favorite food.

MY BIGGEST INFLUENCE

BY ANTHONY JONES

When I was young, my mother tried to get me to do things I didn't want to do. I never really listened because I was little. I always thought that what she was asking me to do was too easy and it would waste my time and hers. For example, she would tell me to throw away my trash or make my bed. I thought that if she could see my trash, she could throw it away. I would only make my bed look messy if I tried to fix it, so I thought she should do it to keep it from looking messy. Now that I'm older, I realize how much work my mother does and I try to do things that she asks for. I believe that my mother is the biggest influence in my life.

My mother is a hard worker. She's shown me what it's like to have to wake up early, go to work, and come home late. She's the only one in the house who works because I'm not old enough and my grandparents are retired. I'm grateful for the things that she taught me. She taught me how life will be later, and how eventually I'll have to get a job to pay for clothes and food for others and myself.

My mother is very smart. She's an accountant, so she works with lots of numbers. I think I'm good at math because of her. I need to thank her for that. I need to thank her for many things: like teaching me life lessons, taking care of me, and being there for me. She also taught me that when I'm an adult, I'll be treated as one;

I'll be respected by some and not by others. She showed me this through her actions.

My mother is unique because she actually knows how to be a parent. There are some people out there who just let their children do whatever they want. My mother allows me to do some things that I like to do, but not everything. She knows that when someone does everything that they want, they can act rude, disrespectful, and crazy. My mother wants me to be nice, respectful, caring, helpful—anything that shows that I am being a good person. Some mothers would buy anything their children ask for because they want their children to be happy, but that just teaches them that you can get whatever you ask for. One weekend I was sick, and I only asked my mother for medicine and ginger ale and she came back with medicine, ginger ale, food, bandages, and new pillows that I really needed. I always had trouble sleeping because my pillows were as flat as a wall and it was really uncomfortable on my head and neck. I slept very well that night because the new pillows were very puffy and comfortable.

When my friend, cousin, mother, and I went on vacation, my cousin told my friend and me that his parents were weird, and that he hates them for that. My friend told him that he needs to love his family and explained why he shouldn't hate his dad. I explained why he shouldn't hate his mother. I told him that she brought him into this world, and although she may be different from others, she will always be his biggest influence. My cousin's reaction was very strange. He looked confused because he knows me well enough to know that I don't normally tell people this type of stuff. I usually talk to my cousin about video games or soccer. I don't think he knew that I was able to talk to him other than through playing video games, but I felt that I needed to tell him, because he would listen to me.

ANTHONY JONES

"My mother is very smart. She's an accountant, so she works with lots of numbers. I think I'm good at math because of her. I need to thank her for that."

My mother is very important to me because she has always been there for me. She jokes with me and she loves me. One time, a soccer player named Luis Suárez bit another player in the World Cup, so I bit my mother's shoulder as a joke and she said, "Get off me, Suárez." That moment was important, because she was taking an interest in learning about the types of things I like (soccer), and she was being funny. To this day, she still jokes about things that I didn't even know she knew about. She sometimes knows things that happened in a soccer game that I don't even know about. A player might score a goal or get injured, or some random, odd thing might happen during a game. One time my mom came home from work and told me that Pierre-Emerick Aubameyang, a player for Borussia Dortmund, scored a goal in the Bundesliga Cup and celebrated by putting on a Spider-Man mask and running around. I was happy that my mother knew the players from my favorite team and what they were doing in their games.

I might have once doubted my belief because there are lots of different kinds of influential people—celebrities, sports stars, and actors—in the world. At one time, I thought that my favorite soccer player, Marco Reus, was the most influential person to me. He's a really nice, cool, chill guy. He's amazing when he's playing soccer with his team. Although he may be a good player, Marco Reus could never rise over my mother when it comes to being my biggest influence. I later realized that he wasn't exactly my most influential person in my life because my mother was. I realized this after she learned about what I like and do. Marco Reus plays professional soccer. My mother plays professional parenting.

When I'm at home, I like to play video games. As it turns out, my mother used to play video games many years ago. She used to play very popular games called Resident Evil. Resident Evil 1, 2, and 3 are my favorite games because you don't just run in and kill zombies. Resident Evil is a game in which you have to make the right moves to survive. One wrong move and you can die. I didn't know about Resident Evil until my mother showed me her Resident Evil game for the PlayStation. My mother and I have a connection to the game. I'm able to make jokes about it and she actually understands what I mean. I feel I am better at the game than my mother, even though she knows more about it than I do. A lot of people say that video games don't benefit you in any way. Resident Evil did benefit me, though, because it helps my mother and me bond.

I realize that most things my mother does for me bring us closer together. I do some things to contribute to that, but everything my mother does helps our family. She does things other parents wouldn't do, but that makes her my mother. Parents don't normally show their children an old video game. She's also made my bed, cleaned my dishes, and thrown away my trash. This has taught me about responsibility. She's helped teach me what it's like to be a hard worker, and how to be respectful. One of the things I like the most about her is that she learns about what I like and how it affects me. She has a good sense of humor. It makes life more fun when I can actually make jokes and she understands and laughs about them.

Micah Chinn is fourteen years old and was born and raised in San Francisco. He has one brother and one sister. He enjoys playing video games and loves playing basketball and baseball. Micah is a true, die-hard Warriors and Giants fan; he celebrated the Giants' World Series win and looks forward to celebrating when the Warriors win the NBA championship. Also, he is left-handed.

DO WELL, BE WELL

BY MICAH CHINN

In the third grade, my belief in hard work was put into action. It was in the early afternoon on a weekend. The sun was shining brightly as my dad brought me to a school yard with my red Mizuno bike. I still couldn't ride it without training wheels or guidance, but that was my goal for this very day. I was excited to accomplish something new. At the yard, I practiced with my training wheels; then my dad took them off and helped me to balance. I fell a few times, and I could feel the hard concrete hitting my skin, but I wasn't going to give up just yet, so I got back up. I could hear my dad saying, "You can do it!" and "Don't give up!" After a few hours of practice, my dad let go of me and I was riding all by myself! I was so happy I could finally ride without help and I'm pretty sure my dad was also. All of this work paid off and I would never forget how to ride a bike after this day. Like me, people who have determination will be successful and accomplish their goals.

For example, Stephen Curry, point guard of the Warriors, has made it very far since he joined the NBA. A couple of years ago Monta Ellis was the star of the Warriors. Everyone had Ellis jerseys in Oracle Arena. Since Monta Ellis left and was eventually traded to the Dallas Mavericks, Stephen Curry has been running the show all by himself. This took determination, hard work, and believing that he could do it. Now Stephen Curry is pretty much the best three-point shooter in the game, and his jersey is the second-most purchased in the world. He was the first player in Warriors history to average twenty-four points and eight assists in a single game. He has a .434 three-point field-goal average per game and tops it off with an average of 35.3 minutes per forty-eight-minute game.

Stephen Curry shares my belief in hard work because he is someone who tries his best all the time. When he trains, it is amazing to watch him. From hallway shots every practice to dribbling between the legs with two balls, it is crazy. He shoots about two hundred to three hundred shots a day and is different from other NBA players because he is the best at three-pointers. Curry made 261 three-pointers in 2013–2014. He probably gets tired of them because he shoots them so much. He is as fast as a machine when he shoots. The reason why he is so good at shooting three-pointers is because he practices them all the time and they are just something he is good at. His father was in the NBA, so his talent could be inherited, but he has certainly developed it on his own, too. Training in the weight room is also very important to him so he can get stronger and make plays easier. There are many different types of training that help Curry to get better. For instance, to develop good hand-eye coordination, he dribbles a basketball with one hand while catching a tennis ball with the other hand. He trains with his coaches and teammates who help give him advice about the game. Training and practicing isn't easy and takes a lot of work and commitment, which I think Curry has.

Training and working hard like Stephen Curry has helped me in a different way. For example, in eighth grade I had this big term project that was a few months of work and was worth a majority of my grade. On top of that, the project had to be at least ten pages and needed an oral presentation with a PowerPoint to go with it. The topic had to be about something in United States history, and

I chose the Korean War because my grandfather fought in it. It was interesting what he had done and how he served in the army. When I got the project assigned in January, I was a little intimidated because the teacher showed the whole class the best projects from last year and a few of them were thirty pages plus! I already knew this was going to be one of the most difficult projects of my life.

In order to try hard and be successful on this project, I had to give up my free time and being able to sleep in because I needed to get a lot of information about the topic from books, online sources, and an interview with my grandfather. He told me that he had to wake up at four or five in the morning for army training, and if he didn't get up, he would get ice water dumped on his head. My grandfather had ten good friends in the war and four were killed. He was also sent to the front line, which made him extremely scared of dying. Battlegrounds reeked of dead bodies and temperatures ranged from zero to one hundred degrees. All of his friends who survived were glad to be alive. My hard work on the Korean War resulted in an A, so I was glad that I had taken all this time to work on the assignment.

Trying hard and being successful can help in almost everything. From playing sports to fighting wars, people can be successful if they work hard. In the future I want to study more about sports. I want to play baseball or basketball in college, but I'm not too sure about professionally because it takes a ton of work to get into the NBA or MLB. If I am committed to sports, I will need to work hard so I will succeed in the future.

Yancy Ame Castro is fourteen years old and from Nicaragua. She is very bright and enjoys creative writing and tutoring other students in all subjects. She wants to go to Stanford to study architecture. She enjoys volleyball and speaks Spanish. If she could have any superpower, she would choose invisibility.

HOW TO MAKE A BETTER WORLD

BY YANCY AME CASTRO

"The happiness you feel is in direct proportion to the love you give." This is an anonymous quote that made me think about how happiness and love are related. I think that these sentiments are related because every time you're happy you have the opportunity to create happiness in someone else's life by showing them love.

I believe that every time you're happy it's because you feel love. One way to obtain happiness is by giving love to people through kindness, consideration, and respect. The way to start showing these things to others is by loving ourselves. If we can love ourselves, then we can make the world happy and can make each other happy. Just by loving ourselves, we can make the world uncomplicated. I think we can mold people into happier human beings by showing them love.

I think love and happiness will always be connected to each other. Without love, you will never know what happiness feels like. There is more than one kind of love. There is friendship, family, loyalty, and self-love and self-respect. I feel that all of these are aspects of love. When I read the quote above, I feel like all my problems have been disentangled. I realize that whenever I'm sad, it's because I'm not giving love to someone, not even myself. Furthermore, I believe that happiness isn't just loving someone else, it's also loving who we are and the decisions we make.

The two people who prove this belief to me the most are my grandpa and my brother, Loquito. My grandpa is a person who can make someone's life really happy, because whenever I see him I automatically smile. Even though he is older, he is always smiling and giving love to those around him. My grandpa is the perfect symbol of happiness because even though he is like a robot (always working), he will always have a smile that lights up everyone's life around him. He is constantly smiling, even when he's sick, just to make people happy. I think every time he is happy it's because he is giving love to others, but also loving himself. He does this by doing the things he loves to do, like working and fixing things. I think what makes him an amazing person is that he gives me part of his small amount of free time just to teach me how to drive or help me with my homework. He helps my mom translate things to English, and for my grandma he cleans their house. I believe that he is an amazing person because even though he is older, it's awesome how at his age he is the embodiment of happiness. I see my grandpa being considerate and kind. I see how that makes us happy, but also makes him happy.

By watching my grandpa, I have come to believe that love and happiness are related. It's important to love ourselves before we give love to others. Loving myself isn't easy because people's opinions make me think that in order to love myself, I have to be perfect. This is impossible because no one in this world is perfect, except God. Loving ourselves, to me, means to love who we are and how we are, without needing to change. I love who I am and that's all that really matters. I believe that if people don't love who they are, they don't really love others. Why? In order to love someone you first have to love yourself. I understand that loving ourselves isn't easy, but it also isn't impossible. I think loving myself is important because if we don't love ourselves, we won't be able to know what happiness feels like. We would treat people how we treat ourselves without love, without consideration, without kindness or respect. This is why loving yourself is important to my belief.

Sometimes my belief is challenged by my brother, Loquito. Loquito does not believe that the world can change and he doesn't think that love exists. He tells me that he has lived a long life even though he is only sixteen years old. He tells me that he gives love to people all the time but doesn't receive it. It hurts me to hear him say these things because he doesn't recognize that he cares about others without caring about himself. It makes me sad to see him angry and miserable because he can't see the positive side to his life. This challenges me because I care about him, and I want him to know what freedom and happiness feel like. I think people should be grateful when someone shows compassion to them. A while ago, I got into an argument about this issue with Loquito. This argument made me really angry because it's really hard to show true love to others, especially if that person doesn't care. It really made me feel miserable because he showed he doesn't care what I think or believe in. This is something we argue about a lot. I don't care that he doesn't believe what I believe. I know this belief is true because I have seen the evidence that proves it in my life.

Between love and happiness there are no differences. They both can make our lives intense, they are both reasons to live, and without them we are not whole. I believe that love is happiness and happiness is love. I believe we all have one true love, but love is not between two people only. Love can be loving something and loving stuff we like to do. The symbol of love is two people loving each other, and that's also happiness. Feeling loved by someone can make us happy in just seconds because if our heart is happy, our minds are going to

"Between love and happiness there are no differences. They both can make our lives intense, they are both reasons to live, and without them we are not whole. I believe that love is happiness and happiness is love."

be happy too. The way I give love is the way I want others to love me. Who I am is the person I want people to love. So make sure every time you say you love someone, be sure about it and how you feel. Feel confident with that person, because that will bring happiness to your life. I believe that being happy is our own choice, because we are the only ones that can decide if we want to love someone. Being loved by someone all depends on our attitudes and how we want to see reality. Love is magic. It can change this world to a better place. If we live with peace and respect, our choices will makes us happy.

Ariana Garth was born in San Francisco. She is fourteen years old. She likes to listen to R&B because she enjoys the beat of the music. At school, Ariana enjoys playing basketball during gym. Her favorite food is her mother's adobo, but she'd like to find some beignets in San Francisco.

LIFE GOES ON

BY ARIANA GARTH

Well, from the first day you're born, you're dying. You're getting older, so therefore, at some point in your life, you're going to be thinking about the things you want to do before you die. The way I imagine death is as if you're in a big room, all the lights are off, and there's no one there with you. Therefore, I believe that people should live life to the fullest, starting the day you're born. I was the same person before I was thinking about this, but now I spend more time thinking about death because a lot of my grandma's friends have been dying lately. I started to think since I only have a short amount of time left before I die, I really want to do the things I want to do.

When I asked my grandma if she misses her daughter and her brother, who both passed away, she says yeah, but at the same time, she says that you can't keep thinking about the past, because at some point in your life someone is going to die. Life will still go on without you, but you will never be forgotten. When someone dies, there will be those people who say, "I'll live for them." Living for someone you've lost could mean living standing up for their name, representing them, and doing stuff they would know is best for you.

So when my grandpa died, he wanted me to stay true to his wishes. He wanted me to get good grades in school and he wanted me to join a sports team. I'm still living up to my grandpa's wishes. He said get good grades and I'm getting good grades. He said to do well in school and I'm doing well in school. Coming up this spring is track and I will try out for it. Outside of school, I like to hang out with my friends and have fun. I am a funny person; I make people laugh. If my grandpa could see me right now, he would be proud of me. I can picture him saying this and smiling. He had one tooth. The doctors gave him dentures but they were uncomfortable and he didn't like wearing them. When he talked, you couldn't see it, but when he smiled, his tooth showed on the bottom. That's when he was happy or when he was laughing really hard. I'm living my life to live up to his wishes, and my life is still going on.

I want to go to Water World before it's too late, before it closes or I die. The first time I went was with my summer program. The second time I went, I went with my best friend Kayla. When I heard where we were going I thought it was going to be a place that makes water coolers. It sounded boring. But when I went, it was totally different. It was like a playground but with water. If you imagine a beach, you think of people in swimsuits and sun, but if you go to Ocean Beach in San Francisco, it's freezing. Everyone is in coats and there's like one dog in the ocean. But Water World was like how you imagine a beach. It was different than I expected and I had fun. It made me think that there are lots of new things that I want to do before I die.

Before I die, here are some of the things I want to do. I want to go surfing because I've never done it, and my mom always says to try new things. I want to go snowboarding because I've only been to the snow one time, and it made me want to go back. The last time I went, I went down the hill on a tube, but this time I want to actually snowboard. If I could travel anywhere, I would go back to New Orleans because I like it there and I love beignets, a deep-fried bread that has a medium spoonful of powdered sugar on it. I went to New Orleans once before when I was in the Junior Olympics, and I think there's more that I could see. I also want to make the Junior Olympics again. To do that you have to come in at a certain place in each competition you do. I would have to join the track team again to do this, and then I would have to qualify. I think I can qualify again because I want to get back in shape and I really love track and field.

If I put my mind to anything, I could probably accomplish it. While my life goes on, I can be focusing on that. Life always goes on.

Lofton Lazar is an avid dramatist and will be playing the role of the butcher, Lazar Wolf, in an upcoming local production of *Fiddler on the Roof*. Lofton prefers tacos to pizza, baseball to basketball, and the Flash over Batman. He shares a birthday with the queen of England and Michael Franti.

I GOT UP AND SHOT ONE OF THEM WITH MY RUBBER BAND

BY LOFTON LAZAR

"Everything happens for a reason." I have been hearing these words all my life, but only recently have I been understanding what it really means. As a young kid I was very mischievous. One very vivid memory I have is of third grade. I was with my friends in our area of the schoolyard and we were hanging out. Back then I always had a rubber band, and that day I was very bored. As these two kids walked by, I had an idea. So I got up and shot one of them with my rubber band. As soon as I did it I knew I had made a really bad mistake. I went to the office at my school and my principal asked me what I was thinking when I did this. In my mind I was saying to myself, *I wasn't thinking anything.* Of course I couldn't say that, so instead I told her that I thought it would be funny. That was better than saying, "I don't know." After this experience I learned to think more about the consequences of my behavior. I didn't want to feel like a dog that pees on the carpet and gets banned to the backyard. You could say this was a pivotal moment in my life. This experience opened my eyes. It made me think about my actions more. This was the start of me starting to realize my belief.

Years later, on the second Friday of my freshman year of high school, I really did not feel like going to school. I was still adjusting from summer. When my dad dropped me off in front of my school I began walking in the opposite direction, straight to the bus stop. I had played hooky from a class before, but this was the first time I cut school. My stomach was queasy as I was going over the situation in my mind. I rode the bus through the Mission and when I got off I started walking to my house. As I was about to go inside I saw my mom's car and realized that she hadn't gone to work. My eyes widened and I knew I should have just gone to school. Instead I sat down at the bench across the street at the coffee shop and waited for her to leave.

After about thirty minutes, I looked up from my phone and saw my mom walking down the street. In all my life I had never seen the face she was making. Her nostrils flared with a big scowl, and her face was red. In that moment I knew I was done. As we made eye contact I could see the anger in her eyes. She walked right up to me and I was speechless. She didn't say anything at first. As we were walking back I was begging my mom not to tell my dad. My mom's silence was like the moment before an archer releases his arrow; it made me worry about what was to come. When she finally spoke she told me that I would not be able to watch TV or use my computer during the school week ever again. I felt as if the arrow only just skimmed me and had broken skin. I was lucky because I knew she was going to take those privileges away but it meant that it would give me opportunities to do other things. In the next few weeks I started making more friends, my grades got better, and I was feeling more confident and being myself.

My mother is a very spiritual person. She is the origin of my belief that everything happens for a reason. She has been telling me this all my life, but I didn't always listen. As I've gotten older and started to experience life more, I've started to understand what she was really saying. Remembering the rubber band incident, or the skipping school catastrophe, has shown me that this belief cannot be understood in one day. It took me almost fourteen years before I could call this belief mine.

In December of 2014, my belief was really put to the test. I flew to Collierville, Tennessee, a few weeks after my aunt passed away to celebrate her life. My mom and my uncle didn't view losing my aunt in a sad, funeral type of way. We all wanted to celebrate the life she lived, not mourn the life she lost. When I first heard that my aunt was sick I was angry and sad. I was angry because she didn't deserve to be sick. I was sad because I was old enough to realize that she was not going to be able to beat cancer.

My aunt was one of the most caring and loving people I knew. She was a pretty wealthy person. I remember that if I wanted something she would get it for me as well as for all my cousins. She did everything she could to make others happy and never did anything for herself. She was always helping others. My aunt and I were very close. We shared the same birthday and she always called to sing me happy birthday; I would sing it back. Whenever my mom and I went to visit we stayed there.

The room my uncle had rented was a huge room for her celebration, enough to fit at least three hundred people. It had tan walls and a chandelier hanging down from the ceiling. In the center of the room was a glass case with my aunt's urn inside. The urn was purple with a beautiful design. As my family and cousins started showing up I got very happy. It was like catching a game-winning touchdown over a guy who is seven feet tall. I hadn't seen some of them in three years. I realized that my little cousins weren't going to come and I understood it was because they were very young and would not have been able to comprehend the situation. As everyone was leaving, my uncle told me that we were going to have a big party at his house the day after. From that moment on, all I could think about was seeing my cousins.

Since my mom and I live on the West Coast I usually feel distant and isolated from the rest of my family. Family is the most important thing in my life. Not being able to see them as much as possible makes it very tough. In these situations, when we all come together, I feel as if we live there.

My mom, my uncle, and I were all patiently waiting for my uncles, aunts, and cousins to arrive. The big dining room with the Christmas tree, covered in purple ornaments, and the paintings reminded me of my aunt. I sat quietly munching on a chocolate cookie my mom had made earlier. In our minds we were also basking in the last silence we would have for a while. As all of my cousins, aunts, and uncles started showing up, I realized that my aunt's passing was bringing everyone together, something that hadn't happened in over two years. As I looked around the room I saw happy faces of relatives. Seeing my little cousins who had grown so much made me realize that this has been hard on all of us, even the little ones. Now that everyone was together and there was love in the air, I realized that having people to go through the pain with makes it a little bit easier. All the love and happiness in the air really made me feel like my aunt's passing happened so that our family could become closer.

My belief is connected to all of these experiences. My first story inspired my belief and opened my eyes to think before I act. My second story was an example of losing privileges but realizing that what I like to do is bad for my grades and keeps me from being more social. Lastly, my third story shows loss of someone I was very close to; yet because I have my belief, it wasn't a completely sad situation. My aunt was the person in the family who got everyone together, and even in the afterlife she managed to get us all together one last time. If other people shared my belief, I think that traditional ways of expressing their feelings could be changed in a good way. I know that keeping a belief is difficult because things may happen that will make me question this belief. Yet if I keep a strong heart and remember my past, I will be able to manage.

Daejah Cummins is a freshman. She was born and raised in San Francisco. She is goofy and loves to laugh as much as she loves shoes!

TO THINE OWN SELF BE TRUE

BY DAEJAH CUMMINS

Everett Middle School was a pretty good school, but the incoming sixth graders had a lot of growing up to do. By the time I got to eighth grade, I could pretty much tell right away who had just come from fifth grade. Some of them were followers—they always tried to be like others, and they would try to do everything the eighth graders did. The hallways would always be loud on the third floor where the sixth graders would be standing in line for class, pushing each other and telling "your momma" jokes. I used to always catch some of them just looking at all the older eighth graders. They would try to sneak into the lunchroom with the seventh and eighth graders. It started to make me think they should be themselves, and stop trying so hard to be like others

One day there was this pretty small, light-skinned girl looking at me through the lunchroom window. It was kind of creepy. When I walked out the door she said, "Hi my name is Emanii!" She told me I was pretty and she asked me to be her "play mom." I didn't know what she meant, but I said, "Sure," because I didn't want to be mean. And she was a good girl; she was smart and sweet. But all of a sudden, during the next few weeks of school she started to act funny and different. One day I heard a loud voice yelling profanities on the second floor where the seventh and eighth graders' classes are. Emanii was with all eighth graders, and she was the only one there who was in sixth grade.

A few weeks later, Emanii's friends came to me at lunch. My friends and I were sitting outside in the yard on the orange benches, eating Hot Chips and Sour Patch Kids, talking about what high schools we were going to attend, what I should do for my birthday, and lots of other things. Emanii's friends came to where we were sitting and one of them called my name, "Daejah, Daejah!" as they were walking toward the orange benches.

I said to my friends, "How do they know my name? I don't know them," sounding all confused.

My friends started to laugh and they said, "I don't know."

The girls got to where we were sitting, and one of them said, "Emanii has been being mean, yelling at us, being rude, and calling us stupid if we got a math problem wrong. But normally she would help us and be in our group."

I told them that I would talk to her about the situation. The bell had rung and I began to walk to my English class on the second floor. I saw Emanii outside of the school. I went up to her and said, "Daughter, come here." When she came over I asked her why she hadn't been with her sixth grade friends and why she was being mean to them. She said that it was because she had new friends. I told her, "Those aren't your real friends. You just met them and you shouldn't trade on your childhood friends for some 'friends' you barely know. At the end of the day they won't have your back the way your real friends would. Those sixth grade girls aren't just your friends, you guys grew up together and your parents are close friends. So you're more like family." She said she knew, and that she missed them. I told her to text them that night and apologize to them.

She said "Okay, thanks," and then gave me a hug.

I believe that people shouldn't try so hard to impress others, because it's not going to get you anywhere. I feel if you want to change yourself, do it because you want to, not because someone is telling you to or you are trying to fit in. I began to feel this way after my experience with Emanii trying so hard to be like her older "friends." She tried acting loud and getting in trouble, when that wasn't her real self. She was really a good person. She was a proper, smart, goofy, fun girl, and I really saw the change in her when she went from being with her childhood friends being with her older "friends." I think you should stay loyal to yourself—but not only yourself, you should also have loyalty toward your real friends.

Always stay true to yourself, especially when you have a decision to make, whether it's good or bad. For example, if it's a situation where you're deciding whether to skip school with your friends and go hang out or stay at school or study for your test tomorrow, do what you think will be most successful and best for you. Even in my own life I have had to make hard choices. I had to choose between being with people I was close to but who would get me in trouble and lead me in the wrong direction, or being with my other friends who would lead me down the right path with school and help me make good decisions for myself. I wasn't really close to them, but in the end, I chose to be with the people who would help me in life and would want to see me doing better than I was before. Now I have become closer to those people. I learned that I have to do what I think will be best for myself.

If you stay true to yourself, it might lead you in a good direction in life. You might even teach your friend how to make better choices, because that's something real friends do.

Victor Melero is a fourteen-year-old who loves to bike around the city, play video games with his friends, and eat barbecued chicken. His favorite spot in the city is Pier 39 because he enjoys playing at the arcade. He especially enjoys the game Cut the Rope, even though it's really difficult.

HARD WORK PAYS OFF

BY VICTOR MELERO

I believe that hard work pays off. I believe that if I try my best, I will get anything I want. I believe that if I work hard, I will succeed in life.

It is challenging to remember my belief when I have to take care of my little brother and sister. It is really difficult because I have to work a lot. I have to feed them, I have to make sure they are quiet in order to help them with their homework, and I have to be a good role model.

Also, I have to make sure my little brother gets what he wants or else I will get in trouble. One time, I had to tell my six-year-old brother, Bryan, and my nine-year-old sister, Evelyn, to take a shower. My little brother, the most annoying little person, refused. It was really hard to put him in the bathtub because he would run away and hide from me. Then time passed and my little brother decided to get in. When it was time to get out of the shower, my little brother had made a big mess. It smelled like stinky feet and Head and Shoulders. Water was all over the place and the carpet was all soaking wet. It made a squeaky noise when I walked on it. That's when I decided to call my mom. I told her what my little brother had done. My brother looked at me with a creepy clown smile and laughed. She started yelling at me saying, "It was your responsibility!" In the moment, this made me think that the work wasn't worth it because I didn't get rewarded. Later on, I realized I was a good role model to my

"In the moment, this made me think that the work wasn't worth it because I didn't get rewarded. Later on, I realized I was a good role model to my brother and sister."

brother and sister. Also, it made me think of my mom and made me proud of helping my mom out. She works hard every day and she deserves the help.

My belief was formed by watching my mom do hard work. When I was a young kid she kept telling me, "When you grow up, you need to work hard and get a good education in order to get what you want." My mom is a hard worker. When I was younger she would always do everything for me. My mom usually wakes me up at 6 a.m. for school and prepares us all lunch. She goes to the grocery store on a daily basis to buy us our favorite meal, called *sopes*. She also picks up my little brother and sister from school. When she gets home she immediately starts to cook and clean the living room. My mom is really tired at the end of the day, but she does this because she wants us to succeed in life. As I get older and start to do my own work, I am realizing how hard it is.

I think everyone should believe that hard work pays off, because some people don't really work hard and in the end they don't succeed. When they do try their best, it pays off. For example, my friend Gloria didn't really care about school. She would just show up and not do anything. After the principal told her she was not going to graduate eighth grade, she decided to work really hard to complete all the missing work. She decided to go to summer school, got her credits, and is now in high school. Gloria worked hard and she succeeded. Her story is proof that hard work pays off.

I recommend you work your hardest, no matter how difficult your obstacles are. You'll be happy you did.

Eva Villareal was born and raised in San Francisco. She is a voracious reader, plays volleyball and soccer, and has collected quotes in a journal since the age of seven. She is shy at first, but she has a goofy side once you get to know her. The middle child of nine siblings, Eva often finds herself in the role of peacemaker.

PUTTING WORDS INTO ACTION

BY EVA VILLAREAL

It was four in the morning when the phone rang. My mom was on the phone for a pretty long time. I could hear her voice cracking. My younger brother Aaron came to my room, panicking, telling me and my sister to wake up and get changed. Now I was panicking. I had this big lump in my throat and I couldn't help but think that something bad was going to happen.

I was in the living room waiting for the rest of my siblings to get ready. In the other room, I heard my older brother Samuel break down in tears. I couldn't help but break down myself because I've never heard my older brother cry so much. My grandfather had been in the hospital for three days. Did all that crying have to do with him?

Let me tell you a little bit about my grandfather. His name was Dr. Samuel Joaquin. My grandfather was a very important person, not only in my life, but in many other people's lives. My grandfather was the leader of my church, The Light of the World. He lived in Guadalajara, Mexico. He was loved by millions of people from all over the world. Everything he did changed people's lives. People from all over the world had something positive to say about his good deeds, not only people from our religion, but worldwide leaders. He was known for his humble heart and for the immense love he had for other people.

Every August, my family tried to make a trip to Mexico to participate in the *Santa Cena*. We gather at the church all dressed in white and participate in the celebration. When my grandfather, the Apostle Samuel, would get up to speak with the church, he would give off a vibe that would make the church feel like anything was possible if you just believed. To me he was not just any ordinary man. All the words that came out of his mouth were words of wisdom.

We rushed to the hospital, got to the tenth floor, and made our way to my grandfather's room. My mom went to speak with the doctors before she went into the room with us. We walked into the room, but no one was in the bed. My heart dropped. I began to think we might have walked into the wrong room. My mother explained that my grandfather knew he didn't have much time left and his wish was to be at home in Mexico when he took his last breath. My grandmother had arranged for him to be flown home.

My family and members from church kept him in their prayers. About a week later, we arrived at church and heard that he had passed away. I felt this emptiness within me, like someone had taken away my heart.

My grandfather taught me to appreciate what you have when you have the chance because you never know when opportunity could be taken from you. When he passed away, I felt like without him nothing was possible, that there was no importance in life if he wasn't around anymore. He told me to try a little harder if I felt like giving up and he also encouraged me to try hard in school. His mind was always set on other people's happiness. He put God first in everything and then he thought of his community. He never thought of himself first.

Days passed and I realized and accepted that he was in a better place. I asked myself, *Would you rather see him happy with God, or see him suffering?*

A week later, I was sitting in the waiting room at the hospital where my mom works. While I was there I was letting things sink in. It took a while to process. I thought, *Have you reached out and grabbed every opportunity that was right there in front of you?*

I started planning on how I was going to restart living my life. I planned to start being more responsible and take things more seriously. For example, I have five little siblings and my mom works six hours a day and my dad works the night shift, so most of the time my siblings and I are at home alone. While my parents are at work, I try to step up and help my brothers and sisters with their homework and do house chores.

There is a time when we have to own up to our responsibilities. Being a student, I need to attend school as much as possible and participate in school activities like sports and studying for the future life that is awaiting me. The choices we make determine the lives we live.

Thinking about my future makes me wonder if I will be able to achieve my goal of becoming a lawyer. As a lawyer I would like to help out undocumented immigrants. Most of these people don't have the right documents and don't have as much of a privilege as I do. They don't get to experience all the things that United States citizens do. My dream is for them to be able to live their life to the fullest, just like I am.

There is not a day when my grandfather's advice does not go through my mind. His words and actions have inspired me to live life like there is no tomorrow. Now I walk with pride, knowing that I'm living up to my potential.

Roldan Jaochico lives in San Francisco and enjoys playing video games and exercising at the gym in his free time. Roldan has a diverse background—his father is Chinese and Filipino, and he recently visited his mother's family in Nicaragua. Roldan also likes science-fiction stories on television and film, and if he could choose any superpower he would have super speed.

LIVE TO HAVE FUN

BY ROLDAN JAOCHICO

When I was little my grandfather Emilio used to take me out to go eat or to go to a park. He was really nice and kind toward me and others, but when I was around ten years old, he passed away and I felt really sad. As time passed by I learned that life goes on and that you have to live it to the fullest. It was easy for me to believe in that because I found it to be really true. Whenever there was a hardship or a challenge in my life, I knew that you just needed to do new things that you have never done before. Because of my grandfather, I now know that life always moves on.

Before my grandfather died, I used to play a lot of video games and I didn't really pay attention to family. I still play them but not as often as I used to because I believe doing other things such as going out to eat or even watching television with family is far more important. If I'm just playing, I'm not really communicating with my family and I know that life is better when you're with a family that cares about you.

Not so long after my grandfather had passed, a good friend of mine went through the same scenario. I met my friend Erman through my mom's friend, and ever since we've been good friends. Erman is three or four years younger than me, and about a year ago his grandfather died. I remember him being really sad, and I felt bad for him because I knew what he was feeling at the time. I tried to help him by telling him that life goes on. And I think that helped him because he stopped crying, and he told me that I was right about living every day to the fullest. A few months later I saw him again and I could see that he looked happier. I was talking to him and he told me that he had recently gone to a boat cruise with his dad and that he had a lot of fun. He also said that he was trying to do new things and did not care about what other people think of him. He then told me that I was a good friend because I had helped him when he was going through a hard time.

The first time I put my belief in to action was about a year ago, when I went with my cousins to the Santa Cruz Beach Boardwalk for the first time. I remember it being a long drive, maybe around two hours. When we parked and got out of the car it was really sunny, and my face got bright red like a tomato. As we paid to get in, I told one of my cousins that all the rides seemed cool because they had interesting designs and they looked big. He told me that we should ride a roller coaster called the Giant Dipper. At first I didn't think it was a good idea because it looked as tall as a skyscraper and I thought I was going to be in great danger. I could fall out of the roller coaster, or even get stuck on it. In the past I probably would not have wanted to ride the roller coaster, but now that my belief has influenced me into doing new things, I need to live my life to the fullest and just have fun.

So I decided to wait in line to get on the roller coaster. While I was waiting I was reading some signs that were there. A few of them had some facts about when the roller coaster was made. When I started to get on the roller coaster I read a sign that said it went fifty-five miles per hour. At that point I was already in the seat and it started to move. I couldn't get off at this point; there was no turning back. The roller coaster started moving up and it started to make a loud clanking noise. I could see the people below me; they looked so small, almost like ants, and all of a sudden the roller coaster went down with a strong force. I could feel air rapidly hitting my face. I started screaming and raising my hands in the air. About a minute or so later the ride ended, and I was surprised that I wanted to ride it again because at first I had felt terrified.

Ever since that day I rode the roller coaster, I felt like I was truly living my life to the fullest. When my grandfather died, it taught me a lesson that life always goes on. So I hope that I do other exciting and interesting things that I've never done before. Because after all, life is short, so just enjoy it as much as you can.

Rogelio Campos is fifteen years old. Rogelio, AKA Ro, enjoys playing sports, especially basketball, hanging out with friends, and likes all things from the '90s. He plans to get cornrows for baseball season, which he hopes will make him run as fast as the Flash.

DO YOU VALUE YOUR LIFE

BY ROGELIO CAMPOS

It was a normal sunny Sunday, and my friend and I were looking for new R&B songs to listen to when it came on: "If You Lose Her" by Joe Thomas! The song made me sad, but then again happy. It sounded like voices talking to you and describing the life they live. The beat was so energetic that I felt like tapping a pencil to the table along with the rhythm! His voice was soft and smooth, and it sounded like he was whispering into my ear. It made me sad because the things he said in that song were so true. *If you lose her, you may not see it now, but when she's gone you'll know how much she's worth.* What Joe is trying to say while singing this lyric is that when you have the opportunity to make something happen, do it—because you won't always have that opportunity; soon it could be gone.

The first time I listened to the song, I didn't really know the lyrics. After a week or so, I began to fall in love with the song, because the soft, smooth voice of Joe relaxed my body. I could really connect to what Joe was saying because in the past I'd had chances to make opportunities happen, but then I lost the chance to do so and regretted it! I started to notice more about the decisions I made in life. Prior to hearing this song, I didn't care as much about choices I made.

One ignorant choice I made in my life was getting cut from the basketball team. On the first day of tryouts I walked into the gym pretty nervous. It was me and twenty-four other students working our butts off to be a part of the basketball team. I could feel my heart jumping up and down and my bones doing the TLC "Creep" dance! While I was nervous, I also had a good feeling I'd make the team. I was so confident when trying out because I thought I was the best player trying out for the team. There was a moment when Coach saw me shoot and I'm guessing he liked the way I shot the ball because he couldn't stop pointing at me.

But sadly, I gave up on the last day because I was lazy and didn't want to go through the hard work anymore. I felt dumb because I always told myself that I would make the team, but I ended up giving up! Instead of going to the last day, I went home sore from two days of tryouts and took a very warm shower. When I got out of the shower I began to ask myself, *Why did I make the decision to not go to the last day of basketball tryouts?*

Now that I think about it, it was just one more day of tryouts. If I had gone I would be on the basketball team! I was so blind. I didn't realize that what Joe said about how "if you lose her you may not see it now, but when she's gone you'll know how much she's worth," was also true in my case: I had the chance to be on the basketball team, but I was so confident that I didn't know what it was worth until I lost it!

A person I know today, who is known as Ape, doesn't value all the things in his life that he should. Ape had the chance to graduate from a public high school, but he didn't value education. It was too late for Ape, and he had to transfer to a continuation school to make up credits. I tried to help Ape by telling him that if he didn't graduate high school he wouldn't accomplish the goals he set as a kid. I feel bad for my friend Ape, because I had the chance to help him before he got sent to continuation school. I also still have a hard time keeping up with my belief all the time.

After I realized the value of joining the basketball team, I then became wiser about choices I made. It was hard for my friend Ape because he wanted to have fun in life and not have to do work. He wanted the easy way in life. My friend was so hardheaded that he believed the world was his. For example, he thought that getting in trouble wasn't important because he wasn't thinking about his future. He was just thinking about what to do to keep himself from being bored. There was a point when I gave Ape advice about doing what he believed in doing, but he didn't listen. Yet to this day I still feel bad because he was a very close friend and could have been happy instead of living with regret.

The famous R&B singer Joe wrote the lyrics that really made me change my perspective in life. Ape and Joe both made mistakes and haven't always valued what they had until all was lost. Like many other R&B singers, Joe shows that he understands he isn't perfect but he knows what he does wrong so he tries to make up for it. His music is credible, because he is honest with his audience by not trying to be perfect. I look up to Joe, because when I need focus in life, his lyrics help center me.

A time when I doubted this belief was when my niece got annoying. I usually play video games or lift weights, so when she came into my room touching everything, she made a huge mess. I got so mad you could see steam coming out my nose and ears, and I chased her so that she would get out my room. One day, while I was chasing her, she fell down. It felt like a San Francisco earthquake, it was so heavy on my heart. Then I realized I should value the time I have with her because she could get seriously hurt at some point, or worse. I don't

"I got so mad you could see steam coming out my nose and ears, and I chased her so that she would get out my room. One day while I was chasing her, she fell down. It felt like a San Francisco earthquake, it was so heavy on my heart."

usually cherish the time I have with her, but that one day when she fell down really made me think about how much she's worth!

It took me a while to fully accept the belief that you should value what you have before it's too late and no longer have the chance to value it. I value this belief because of when I got cut from the basketball team. Thinking about it really gets me emotional because I had the chance to do something that I love, but lost the chance to do that by not going to tryouts. I begin to get mad at myself when I think back to that day. But mistakes motivate me. Today this belief has inspired me to try out for the baseball team and give all my effort, even if it means being sore and tired. My plans for the future are to achieve the goal of making the basketball team next year so that I can play in the NBA when I get older, and prove to myself that anything is possible if you value it.

By the way, Joe, if you're reading this, I just want to say that you're an underrated R&B artist and I really hope to meet you someday!

Robert Lee III is fourteen and a four-sport athlete who proudly wears size thirteen shoes. A San Francisco native, Robert also lived in Georgia for about two years. He is a loud, goofy person, but an excellent student.

BE GRATEFUL FOR WHAT YOU'VE GOT WHILE YOU'VE GOT IT

BY ROBERT LEE III

My belief is that life is too short. I believe this because my father died suddenly when I was five years old. Suddenly, there was no other man in the house—I was the man. I washed dishes and I had responsibilities when I was young, like watching my little sister and also making sure no man was coming in the house who I didn't approve of.

My father was tall, six foot four, and very athletic. He played basketball, football, and baseball. He was very buff and could bench press five hundred pounds. He was bald with brown eyes. Always a stylish dresser, he worked construction and also at a gym. He coached a basketball team. He had two children he loved, my sister and me.

I was five years old. One day my mom picked me up from George Washington Carver Elementary School and took me to get some ice cream. She told me the terrible news while I was sitting in the backseat. My father had just been shot on Third Street and Palou, and he didn't make it. I was very angry, but I did not cry. I felt like a grown man when I was five. She took me to the movies, and then we went to get my sister from school and told her the news. My grandmother came over to the house that night and talked to my mother. I then went to sleep because I didn't want to think about it.

A couple days later, the fact that my dad was gone kicked in, and then I started to remember things. I remembered how I used to wake up in the morning and how we would eat breakfast together. Then one day, all of a sudden, he wasn't there to eat breakfast with me. Kids at school used to play around and make fun of each other by talking about "your mama" or "your dad." Whenever kids made fun of my father, I went crazy and started fighting them. I remember now I fought one boy outside, but we were so young we didn't even know how to fight. We grabbed each other and rolled on the ground. I got on top and swung, and then he got on top and hit me. We had gone behind a corner so the teachers couldn't see us, but they heard kids yelling so they came and broke up the fight. While a teacher pulled me away, I was still trying to go after him, yelling, "Let me go." The teacher grabbed me, got down on his knees, and told me that I had to calm down. He said he knew how I felt, but I couldn't take it out on people like this. At the time, I was so frustrated that I wasn't listening. After I calmed down a little, I got what he was saying.

My mom also tried to talk to me. One day, my mom had a talk with me, and she said I had to let things go. My father was gone and would never come back and I had to get over it. She said I had to stop making trouble and accept the fact that life was just too short. I was angry that he was never coming back because I used to write about how he was my motivation in life and how, when I make it all the way some day, he was going to get half of whatever I got. I wanted to get him whatever he needed. Even though my mom tried to talk to me, I still didn't really understand what she meant about how short life is.

I moved to Atlanta, Georgia, when I was around six. Atlanta was hot, with too many bugs. After living in Georgia for two years,

"He took me under his wing like I was one of his sons and he became a father figure to me. My godfather is like the boss."

I moved back to San Francisco and met up with my godfather, the black side of the family. He took me under his wing like I was one of his sons and he became a father figure to me. My godfather is like the boss. I hung out with him and went around the city and started doing things again. He got me into football and I played for the Brown Bombers of Hunter's Point. He's my mom's cousin. The sons of my godfather, I'Jah and U'Jah, are some of my best friends. They play basketball with me.

My godfather told me that life was short and I can't be on the streets, smoking weed and messing with guns, or I'll end up in jail or six feet under. I started looking around and realizing how many people were dying at a young age, how many kids my age and younger were losing their mom or their dad. There is enough sadness going around. This makes me think that I should stop getting in trouble and listen when somebody tells me something because they are most likely right.

Two years ago in middle school, my friend Buddha was going down the hill to fight another boy names Los. Los was mad because Buddha had taken his girl. Buddha was beating Los; he was on top of Los punching him. I had been watching the fight and decided that it should be over. I grabbed Buddha off of Los and said, "Bruh, it's over with." Buddha started to walk away but Los yelled out that he wanted to fight again. Buddha said, "No, I already won." Los said, "All right, next time I see you alone, I'ma shoot you." Walking back towards Los, taking off his backpack, Buddha said, "What did you say?" I grabbed Buddha and told him, "Forget about it bruh, life is too short." Buddha knew what I meant and said, "All right." We grabbed his stuff, walked down to the T train, and went to Jo Lee Basketball Gym. The reason I gave Buddha that advice is because he is like a brother to me. His dad takes time out of his day to work out with my friends and me. The reason he takes that time is because he lost a couple of friends and family to the streets and he doesn't want to lose us.

I believe that life is too short, but I don't know if other people have this same belief. Because of this belief, I act smarter about the things I do. I pay attention to the people I hang around and the decisions I make every day. I try to stay at school more rather than going straight home. I have an advantage over some other kids because I'm great at sports.

Life is too short to be doing dumb things, hanging out on the street, and wasting time when you could be in school getting an education and playing sports. You can get money from playing sports instead of trying to get money on the streets.

Because life is so short, you should get a job at an early age, or help your community out. Start a garden project. Clean up the community where you live. Put up money for the things you need to make your community better. I try to spend more time in the gym and at school. I try not to go home because if I am at home for a long time I would want to go outside and hang with the guys. I know they will end up doing the wrong things and I can get into trouble.

Because life is too short, don't be ungrateful for your family. Your family might only be there for a little bit of time, so if they tell you something it's for a good reason. My dad told me to always respect my sisters, even when they get on my nerves and irritate me. He said, "You wouldn't want some random dude disrespecting them, so you should treat them right and make sure your friends treat them right." I'm grateful that he gave me this advice. Without that, I would always joke around and talk about people.

Life is short and sweet, so make the most of it. I will.

SMALL ACTS
OF BEAUTY

STORIES OF ONE PERSON VS. THE WORLD

Vanessa Lopez was born and raised in San Francisco. She likes to read and write poetry. Her favorite foods are pizza and sushi. She enjoys traveling and exploring new places. Vanessa cares deeply about the little things in life.

PEACEFUL LIVES

BY VANESSA LOPEZ

I try to make the world better in my own small way. I garden a lot; I've planted a few lemon trees and harvested the lemons to make guacamole. Lemons are like the color of sunshine; they are smooth and round and cold to the touch, but when you cut them open the citrus scent and the sour juice feel and taste like the energy of the sun.

I also take care of roses in my backyard; I prune them and pick them to put in a vase in our home. The roses are so elegant with their big, soft, curvy petals. My roses are the color of snow. I have been gardening since kindergarten. I even started to save money for buying my own gardening supplies. Through gardening I make the world more beautiful.

When I garden or plant something, I feel calm and positive. I know that I'm helping something grow and live. The soil is welcoming and harmless, with a texture of moist, shredded wood, grainy and warm. When I am planting I make tiny holes and, after burying the seeds, I drizzle a gentle waterfall of water. When I am outside tending to my garden I feel the power of the elements—a cool breeze of passing wind, warm rays of sunlight. Sunshine gives food to the plants, and it makes life possible. I like paying attention to the natural wonder in the world around me; it makes another day possible and gives me strength when I am going through hard times.

I remember watching my uncle go through a hard time in his life. He used to always watch the news, which is full of negativity, and he was also worried about making money for his family. He worried about a lot of things and brought that attitude to everything he did. Then, one day, my dad talked to him and told him, "The world is made messy through our own actions in our own homes." He taught my uncle and me that day that each one of us can make the world more broken or more beautiful. It is up to us.

After that I noticed that my uncle became more observant and had more perspective. He would pay more attention to his wife and children. They used to visit my home acting negatively, but later they became more open and positive. Now my uncle is no longer talking about what worries him, and he seems relaxed and peaceful all the time. It was very meaningful for me to watch this change and I learned that I don't need to worry; I can appreciate each new day.

Watching this change in my life was like a flower beginning to bloom. I was very excited when this all happened and I was also afraid that it was fragile and might fall apart. If you don't water flowers, they will get dehydrated and lose their color. If you don't feed plants with the necessary nutrients and nourishment, they get weak and the stems begin to bend. The roots come out of the ground and the plant dies. If you don't have a positive attitude in life, it is similar to what happens to the plant. Having a positive attitude adds nourishment and vibrant color in our lives. Having a negative attitude is like losing feeling and love. Not having peace with yourself or with your life is like the dying plant, where enjoyment in life is gone.

Feeling positive is one way we can make our homes better. Being mad at one another and having strong, blind feelings creates so many terrible things in our world. Worrying about every little thing doesn't help either, so finding ways to remain calm and positive is important. Often people overreact about the small things, and I think that gets in the way of living in beauty and strength. Small acts of beauty matter in a big way by making everyone around you notice and keep in mind the caring and the importance in it.

I believe that we affect the world around us through our every thought and action and that every small act of beauty matters. Each act can change us. We are responsible for our little creation of peace and beauty, which motivates us to care for it. We might do regretful things to our own lives, but the beauty of life is in growing. If we plant a little seed in our minds and our gardens, it will grow and become beautiful, and all the tending and hard work will make it possible to believe. Making this happen is like believing what I believe.

Kenan Mirou grew up in Syria. When he was thirteen his family moved to San Francisco. He has one older brother and one older sister, only one of whom likes his music. Kenan is an EDM DJ, and he helped grow the DJ club at Mission High School. He has plans to go to medical school someday.

THE STORY OF MY LIFE

BY KENAN MIROU

I have never actually met someone with the same story as mine. What I had to go through might not be the toughest, but it definitely impacted my life in such an insane way and taught me so many lessons. I had to be and act like an adult because my life was going to run me over if I didn't. It's not easy to develop your thinking and act like an adult when you're really just a ten-year-old, but luckily I had the right people who supported me throughout my whole life. I believe that if you have the right amount of positive energy and a strong source of support, then you will be able to face any difficulty.

A year after my parents were officially divorced, my siblings and I started noticing that my dad was seriously overwhelmed. Coming home after work, he would go straight into his bedroom and would respond to all of our questions with, "I don't feel like talking." Juggling the responsibilities of his work, health, and children, it seemed like he had to deal with everything by himself. One day, he told us he couldn't give us a ride to school because he had an appointment. Right away, I knew that it was something that had to do with his health. As expected, there was something wrong. He was told that he had lymphoma, cancer of the lymph nodes.

That moment was the start of a mysterious, terrible, and back-breaking journey. He tried his best to hide it from us, but it was more than obvious that something was up when I saw my father looking down, frowning, and packing his suitcase, with big stacks of money being carried in a separate bag. He told us he had a project in Germany, but of course we figured out later that this money was going to be used for treatment. Before he left, while my brother, sister, and I were in the airport, he told us, "I have always been that wall in your life that you lean on when you're tired or feeling any weakness, but now, I'm sorry I can't be that wall anymore." When he said that, I felt abandoned; we had already lost our mom and now my dad was telling us that the only good thing left in our life, our father, was no longer able to be there for us. At this moment, my belief was born; I knew we had to stay strong.

While my dad was away, we stayed at my auntie's house and we were absolutely devastated. As hard as it was, I knew I was the one who had to get up, wipe off my siblings' tears and my own, and just deal with this tragedy, even though I was the youngest one in my family. While packing our clothes to go to my auntie's, I saw my siblings, silent and despairing. I told them, "We have an amazing father who has been supporting us in such a phenomenal way since the day we were born. Now when he needs us to utilize his support to stay strong, we just put him down? No, we should never show any weakness; we got this." My brother and sister didn't say anything, but their mood rose a little and I could see a little spark of motivation in their eyes.

It's crazy that all of a sudden, we had to worry about things that we never thought would be a problem. At times, I felt like it was too much and I kept asking myself and the world, *What did I do to deserve this?* Even in these dark moments, I still felt some strong support come from inside that felt really close to having my dad around. The strength I suddenly acquired at that moment came from my belief. I realized that dealing with my dad's illness was not the first time I had to rely on my belief. I had actually spent nights thinking about this belief from the moment my mom left the house.

Not having our mother around was a huge gap in all of our lives that we were surprised we were able to fill in. I was the only person at home when the last argument between my parents happened. I was the only one to witness my mom having to leave everything behind in a matter of minutes. I couldn't believe that, after that, she wasn't able to spend time with us. That day, I felt like punching my dad, but I somehow found myself hugging him. Maybe I knew he was already going through too much to have to deal with his son crying, or maybe I hugged him because I felt like he was the only good thing left in my life. I also realized that I was hugging him because I felt like that was the time for me to become that support he needed in that heartbreaking moment. This was my belief, before I even knew it, because I was the one who had the power to support my father when he had lost his power momentarily.

He was gone in Germany for about three months and when my father came back, he had totally changed. A large group of our family, about twenty people, met him in the arrival terminal of Damascus International Airport. He had totally lost the hair on his head and some of his eyebrow hair too, so we barely recognized him. We grabbed his suitcases from him and went back to our house. We've always had this thing in my family where if my dad wanted to talk about something important, he would call all of us up to a specific room in the house to talk about whatever was up. When all of the extended family had left, he did that exact same thing and he was totally straightforward with us. "I obviously lied to all of you. I went to Germany knowing that I was getting chemicals put in my body and honestly, I wasn't even sure that I was coming back."

At that moment, I had a moment of realization that really made sense of everything that had been going on throughout those specific two or three months. I was actually able to be the replacement for my dad when he was gone. I had enough strength and hope to keep my family standing after it had been missing one of its most important pieces for a long period of time.

I couldn't have been more proud of myself. Out of my whole family, even while being the youngest, I was in fact the person credited for being that crutch that kept the family up at the right time. I was right when I said that I believe if a person has the right source of support and the right amount of positive energy, then he is ready to face the entire world with all its obstacles without even worrying about breaking down at any moment. My mom and dad had been supporting me my whole life. While they supported all of my siblings, they supported me the most because of a medical condition I have grown up with and because I am the youngest. The care and love I received from my parents throughout my whole life was the fuel I used when I had to step up and be the biggest source of support for my siblings and my father. My belief isn't a small thing. It was my only key for a better life. I'm pretty sure if I didn't have the belief and if I didn't share it with my family, we would have been in such a different condition and our family would have been considered "weak" or "collapsed."

There's a pretty funny thing about my story. In Arabic, my name, Kenan, means a strong cover that keeps people warm and protected. It can also mean a weapon that is used in the time when it's really needed. My parents gave me my name and provided me with all I needed in order to live up to it.

"I had to be and act like an adult because my life was going to run me over if I didn't."

Andrea Ayala was born in El Salvador. Her most vivid memory of her time there happened at a waterpark and involved turtles, an ostrich, and an alligator. When she was eight, she moved to San Francisco, where she now lives in the Bernal Heights neighborhood. She has a five-year-old sister named Giselle and is especially proud of her prowess in the game Far Cry.

TO TAME A FEAR

BY ANDREA AYALA

I believe that fear is an illusion. When I was about eleven, I watched a movie called *V for Vendetta*, and it really changed the way I thought. There was a scene in the movie where a woman named Evey told V, an anarchist who saved her from an attempted rape, that she was always afraid. She didn't like that about herself. When V heard that, he wanted to help her and make her fearless. V kidnapped her but didn't tell her it was him. She thought it was other people who were trying to get V. He put Evey in a locked room, cut her hair, dragged her, and burned her with hot water. During this time Evey found herself becoming more and more brave. When her captors demanded, "Tell us where he is or die," she responded, "I'd rather die." The moment she said this, she was released. It turned out that she was never actually captured; it was all a test of bravery. She would have felt vulnerable and meaningless if she had let her fear take over. She chose to not let fear control her.

I can relate to this belief because I have faced fear and was able to pull myself together.

I was in eighth grade at Paul Revere School, and it was the first year that we had electives. There were four electives you could choose from: drama, chess, EPGY (learning computer activities), and algebra club. I chose drama club because it seemed fun and playful. The elective was about five weeks long, and in the first two weeks we did activities to get comfortable and really get to know our classmates. Then our drama teacher introduced us to the play *The Taming of the Shrew*. This play was about a man, Petruchio, who thought he could control women. There were two sisters. One was humble and sweet, and the other was stuck-up and mean, but witty. He ended up with the witty one, and tried to "tame" her and outwit her. When my teacher picked the main and minor roles, I was chosen for the main role, Petruchio, who appears in every scene! Me! I was so overwhelmed and scared.

Our teacher made us do run-throughs of scenes and sometimes the whole play. I hadn't memorized my lines yet, so every time we did the run-throughs, I was unprepared and took the rest of my classmates down with me, like I was the Titanic. My teacher started getting mad; her eyes would widen, infuriated over my carelessness. When our performance time came, I wanted to really apologize and make it up to her. I found out my mother was going to be watching in the audience and I wanted to make her feel proud. Determined, I put in the effort and started finding other ways to memorize my lines. One way was to record myself saying the lines and listen to them back, like memorizing my favorite song. I realized that my fear of failing had been keeping me from learning the play. I hadn't wanted to freeze onstage and ruin the play because I didn't remember a line. But then in my head I said, *Fear is an illusion and it's blinding you.* I began to calm myself and really get the play into my system.

On performance day, right before we started, I was backstage. Petrified and insecure, and feeling like a mouse confronted by a cat, I kept telling myself, *It's okay, it's okay,* and practicing the opening lines in my head. I had my trustworthy iron sword resting in my holster. My classmates were surprised that I seemed so calm and ready on the outside, but I was really very anxious and scared.

The more I saw my classmates sweat and shake, the more I didn't want to be like them. As I saw them freaking out, I realized fear was destabilizing them. I knew I was stronger than they were. As the curtain call approached, I became calmer and calmer because I knew I was no longer afraid to fail.

My part was after the sisters' scene, and I was ready to say my lines. As I stepped onstage, I felt a sense of relief because I felt confident, even though this was a completely new experience. One of the lines from my first scene was "Villain, I say, knock me at this gate, rap me well, or I'll knock your knave's pate." In this line, I was calling my servant stupid for thinking that "knock" meant to fight. Each line I said had a little humor, and the crowd clapped and laughed each time. The laughter made me feel a rush of euphoria and confidence. By the last scene I was so relieved and felt accomplished, satisfied with my performance. When my costar and I walked to take a bow, we heard the applause getting louder and louder. It escalated to yelling, like maxed-out volume on speakers. I knew I did so well; I was going to be congratulated with chocolate ice cream my mom would buy for me. My incredible performance was a reflection of me setting aside my fear. Seeing my mom and teacher smile and clap was worth all my mental distress.

If the world knew or understood that fear is an illusion, there would be more freedom in people's minds. Fear acts like a rusty jail cell, restricting us from what we really want to say or do. When we understand that fear is just something that's stopping us, we can begin to let go and change for the better. The better in this case would be to free your mind and yourself. I believe that when one really understands that we are being held back by fear, then we are free of the illusion.

Carlos Hernandez was born in San Francisco. When he's not on his track bike, he'll be out and about in the city. His favorite quote is, "Never give up on a dream just because of the time it will take to accomplish it; the time will pass anyway." If he had $1,000, he would drive to Long Beach to cruise with his friends.

LOOK OUT

BY CARLOS HERNANDEZ

Skating down a hill, cruising like I do on a normal day, I could hear the wind hitting my face. Then out of nowhere, I saw a car. The car door was open and I had to go around it. All I remember is landing on my arm extremely hard and then getting up fast, holding my arm…

Skating takes patience. It takes work and thinking that you want to get better. You have to think about what to do to get yourself better, what you need to work on, and what needs to be left behind. If you have fear, and if you don't overcome that fear, you won't make any progress. For example, I just got back on my board after taking a huge break and it's not the same as it used to be. I can't do the same tricks I knew and I don't feel comfortable anymore. Going off stairs and doing flat tricks isn't the same because fear is keeping me from doing those things. *Flat tricks* means doing a trick on flat ground, like an ollie (a simple jump) or a pop shuv.

I believe that being successful takes work. My dream is to finish high school, and although my days at school are not always the best—sometimes they are good, bad, or boring—I always manage to get through it. In my mind I'm always thinking about what to do after school, thinking of all the crazy and fun things I'll do. But first I have to put the hard work into school. At the end of the day, I realize that I'm in control.

Looking back, when I was in middle school, I wasn't as positive. I was a whole different person. I hated school and I didn't like attending it, so I just wouldn't go. Even if I did want to go to school, I just wouldn't do work if something was hard. I would just leave it and not do anything. But at the same time, that brought trouble and that had to change. Trying to get back into school wasn't the same, and I had to build all of my skills back, which took a lot of time.

I didn't have anything to call it back then, but now I call it reflection. I knew I had to make a change if I wanted a better life. Now I am able to take more responsibility for my actions and the person I want to be. I take care of myself and my business.

At the end of the day, skateboarding is similar to my high school experience in the choices and independence they both require. There is a certain momentum when you take off on whatever trick you're doing. *One, two, three*...my foot pops the board hard and my front foot slides, lifting the board evenly off the ground, a concert of clapping boards as skaters land hard on the ground echoing around me.

Both skateboarding and school require momentum to be completed. You have to keep going, even if you are having a hard time, and keep trying. If you've ever fallen or gotten injured from a skateboard, you will understand not only the rush of pain but also the urge to get back up and try the trick again. The need to feel like you achieved something during a "session" is a feeling most skaters talk about.

A couple years ago, when I broke my arm, it took a while to get back on my board and it didn't feel the same. After my cast was sawed off, tiny impressions remained, and my arm looked wasted and weak. As the time passed, the arm got stronger and stronger by itself. Even though my arm was broken, it actually made me a stronger skater inside. At the end of the day, any challenge you face is ultimately with yourself and your beliefs.

CARLOS HERNANDEZ

Now I've learned that you have to overcome your fears if you want to get where you want to be. One of my favorite quotes, which I saw on a profile on Instagram, is, "Life is like the ocean; it can be calm or still and rough or rigid. But in the end, it's always beautiful." To me, this means that life can be hard sometimes and it won't always be easy. There will be a lot of ups and downs, and you will have to manage to go through it. So I'll continue to get back on the board, no matter what, because you never know when you'll land that trick.

Kevin E. Guzman is fifteen years old. He was born in Honduras and has one brother and one sister. These are some things about Kevin you might want to know: he has swag, he has a dog named Mia, and he may or may not have a sixth toe.

IT'S A SUPERPOWER

BY KEVIN E. GUZMAN

When I was in the first grade, my teacher told me that I had ADHD. I thought it was homework. I was sitting in class as Mr. M walked toward me. I was able to smell the pancakes he was making in the back of the class. The pancakes smelled like smooth butter and very nice, warm dough. In a somewhat sad voice, he told me that I had a condition. He said my condition meant that I couldn't sit still or concentrate as easily as others. He also told me that I was not able to sit still for a pretty long time. All of the students in my class heard Mr M and started laughing. Then he told the students to stop yelling or he would not give us pancakes. And little tiny me was wanting to be cool so I yelled, "Yeah, what he said!" After all that, he told me it was called ADHD. The students didn't know what ADHD was, and I didn't either. The kids stopped playing with me and called me a bunch of mean and rude names.

One week later, I was lying on my white comfy couch thinking about what Mr. M told me in class. I told my mother about the disorder the teacher told me. And she explained to me that it was just a thing that makes it hard to sit still and concentrate. I was confused about the way this felt. Then she told me, "ADHD is not a disorder, it's a superpower."

I went to school the next day and explained what ADHD was to my classmates. They didn't care and started laughing more, so I told the teacher, and he explained it to my classmates. The kids in my class felt ashamed and wanted to be my friend. I said no because I didn't like them, and I just continued with my life. I was thinking that I didn't need rude and mean people in my life. I was also thinking about what my mom would be making for dinner when I got home.

A couple days later, I was playing at my school using the monkey bars. I was swinging toward the middle bar. While I was reaching the bar, I touched it and my hand slipped. I fell on the ground and landed on my back. While I was on the ground I started thinking about what my mom had said about ADHD while the pain was going away. I thought that I would be in a lot of pain, but I wasn't. I got right back up, and I really felt like ADHD was a superpower. When I got up and saw the teachers run toward me, I was standing proudly. And then, when the teachers saw me get up and run back toward the monkey bars, they were surprised like I was. Maybe they thought that I was a superhero, which is what I thought.

A time when I put this belief in action was about two or three months before I started high school. At my middle school over the summer, there was a skateboarding competition. It was statewide. I have never seen so many people sign up for a competition. It was the third round and there were five rounds in total. My brother was in the first, my friend Chris was in the second, and I was in the third. I was surprised that my brother was in first place for two rounds. My turn was sneaking up on me and I was trying to fight it off. I started to think negatively about falling or messing up on a trick. But then my mind flew away and I remembered what my mom told me in the first grade. Then I was ready. As the DJ was yelling my name, I was able to hear all the people in the crowds cheering for me. That made me happy. As I rolled out, I was pumped up as I was going up for my first trick, a five-stair kickflip, and I landed it with ease.

I think that it is not cool that there are no songs or movies that talk about ADHD. I think that Michael Bay needs to make a Transformers movie and make a car have ADHD. That would be cool. Another question is, why would there ever be a movie about ADHD? I think that most people think that ADHD is not anything important and think that it's a little cough or a small flu. But people get ADHD for life; it's not a little two- or three-day thing. It's forever. And sometimes it can mess people up very bad.

Now I know that I am not the only one with ADHD, and I was right—it is a superpower. This sends a message to other people, just because I have a disorder does not make me any different from any other person. I am still the same person inside and out. Now I am in the ninth grade at Mission High School. I have not changed at all, not one bit. I am awesome, I can bake, cook, and skateboard. I am on the school baseball team. I love to play video games like there's no tomorrow. ADHD is attention deficit hyperactivity disorder and it means, for example, that I cannot sit straight for a long period of time. And just because I have this thing does not make me any different from anyone else.

Jose Rodriguez has lived in San Francisco for as long as he can remember. He dislikes sad movies, like *Boyz n the Hood*, and when he was a kid, he was "destroyed" by *The Lion King* when Mufasa died. He likes staying at the house and taking it slow while snacking on Nutella and toast. He frequently uses the word *bruh*, but only because it got implanted in his brain from hearing it so much.

WHEEL OF FORTUNE

BY JOSE RODRIGUEZ

Have you ever had the feeling that you didn't have full control over your life? You do your best, try your hardest, and do all you can, but still fail to succeed. It feels like life is a wheel of fortune and although you just spun it with a high probability of success, you were unlucky and the wheel landed on failure. Sometimes life is out of your control and you have to hope that the best will happen.

"Life is a wheel of fortune. It's your time to spin it." This line came from Tupac Shakur, one of the greatest figures in rap. The phrase struck me because even though you try to be the captain of your own life, there are many things in this world that will be out of your control. However, this is balanced out by things that are actually under your command.

When I was applying for high school, I felt my life was a little out of my control, like a car drifting out of control in a blizzard. I wanted to go to Lincoln, but was enrolled at Mission High. Throughout the first half of my eighth grade year, Lincoln was my aim and preferred school. I remember sitting on my desk next to the window, feeling the bright sun, when my social studies teacher said that there is a low probability that someone can enroll at Lincoln, because it is the first choice of students at half the middle schools in San Francisco. When he said that, the warmth of the sun faded and was blocked by a dark gray cloud, like my hopes for going to Lincoln. Most of my friends also had their eyes set on that school, which gave me even more reason to pick Lincoln. If I were to get into Lincoln, I would go to the school I wanted and I would maintain strong friendships. From the group of friends I had, I was the only person that ended up attending Mission. At the time, I worried that all the friendships I struggled to build would be over and I would have to start from scratch.

In the final days of my eighth grade year I was playing basketball with some friends during PE in my middle school's North Gym. We were having an intense three-on-three game. The game lasted the whole period. As I jumped to get a rebound, a ball rolled under me from another game. I had no control over how I would land. I ended up landing on the side of the ball and when I hit the floor, I went ankle first to the floor. I lay on the floor for a good ten to fifteen minutes. I felt the excruciating pain from my ankle soaring up my leg to my knee. My vision went bad. I started to see little black dots everywhere. At the time, it seemed like it was endless and that the pain would last forever in a concentrated point on my ankle. When I opened my eyes, I saw one of my friends reaching out for my hand so that he could help me up. When he helped me up, I had to balance myself on one leg. My ankle was weak and in so much pain that I was barely able to limp. My friend helped me to the elevator. On the way there I kept on apologizing because I was putting so much weight on his shoulder.

In this case, the spinning wheel was me starting the game of basketball. The wheel itself landed on an unfortunate event, which was spraining my ankle. The ball that came rolling under me was out of my control like many things are in life. But although I sprained my ankle, and I'm not that good at basketball, it didn't stop me from wanting to keep playing. When the wheel lands on an unfortunate event you have to hope for the best and keep spinning.

The belief that life is a wheel of fortune comes from something that is larger than just my life. In the movie *Batman Begins*, Bruce Wayne had no control over his fear of bats. This led to Bruce wanting to leave a play because in one part of the performance there were shadows cast in the form of bats. Bruce had no control over his fear and panic. He rushed out of the theater with his parents. They rushed toward an exit that led to an alleyway. What happened in the alleyway forever changed Bruce: both of his parents were shot and killed by someone who was desperate and wanted some money to keep on moving on. Bruce started to become someone who wanted to protect those who couldn't defend themselves. The tragic event in the alleyway was bad luck that changed Bruce for the better. Bruce kept on spinning the wheel by training. He became someone who was willing to put his life on the line for the weak. Bruce Wayne became Batman. He became something bigger than he had hoped.

Life can be out of your control. The harder you try to control it, the harder it will be to accept the fact that there are many things out of your reach. Even though some things are out your control, there are also many things that you are able to control in your life. No one decides what you are going to have for breakfast or what friends you can and can't have. The events that I have shared portray how control in your life is balanced out like the yin and yang in ancient philosophy. Although it seems that I'm saying life will always be random, like Batman overcoming his fear and using it to make himself stronger, the random events and the events that are under your command will be balanced out.

LaCharles "Cheeko" Wells is a freshman at Mission High School. He is fifteen years old and was born and raised in San Francisco. Cheeko's favorite food is pizza topped with cheese and barbecued chicken. If he could have any superpower, Cheeko would opt for superspeed so he could travel fast.

YOU ALWAYS HAVE A CHOICE

BY LaCHARLES "CHEEKO" WELLS

Growing up, I saw people dying for no reason, trying to be what they were not, and thinking they were about that thug lifestyle. This kind of thing happens all the time, and here's one way it could go down.

Imagine a guy my age, someone I know. We'll call him Troy. He moved into the hood, so he chose to adapt to all that hood stuff. He started ditching school, smoking weed, posting on the corner, selling dope, and throwing up gang signs at people. I knew that wasn't him at all, but it seemed like he was becoming one of them.

As he started ditching school, his grades began to drop. His GPA was under a 0.60. His mom confronted him, and as always, he ran away from his problems. One day, he and his friends went for a drive. Troy thought they were just going to chill out and hang somewhere, but his friends had different plans. His friends secretly plotted a drive-by, starring him as the shooter.

The car stopped at the corner. Instantly they saw their victim. The driver pulled out a Glock 40 from the glove compartment. Troy's heart stopped for a second. He wiped his eyes so he could see clearly.

"What, you never seen a gun before?" the driver said.

Troy paused and swallowed fear. "Yeah, I have."

But everyone in the car knew he was lying. So the driver said, "Huh. Take the gun, then." Troy's eyes glowed.

"For what? I don't wanna go to jail, you crazy?"

The driver said, "We going for a drive-by!" He tossed Troy the gun carefully. Nervously, Troy caught the gun, reckless.

"You ready?"

Troy rubbed it, feeling power through the gun, staring at the extended clip hanging from the bottom. Troy replied, "Yeah, just do this."

The driver turned off the lights and was starting to creep up at the victim, who was smoking. As soon they got five feet away from him they began to roll down the window. Troy cocked back the gun and, as his hand filled up with regret, he let out two shots. BOW BOW. They sped off yelling with joy, with big smiles on their faces. Troy just said, "Yeah man, let's get back to the hood so I can go to the bathroom."

As they dropped him off they yelled "Troy with da 40!" Troy smiled, then ran to his bathroom. As soon as he got there he threw up in the toilet, stomach filled with fear, regret, and stupidity. Troy was throwing up guilt. As he walked to his room, the gun fell out of his jacket and his heart dropped. He quickly called his friends, but they didn't pick up the phone.

The next morning he woke up and it was all over the news. He started to feel the pure pressure of the night before. His mom walked in his room.

"Troy, did you see the news? There was a homicide drive-by last night."

He swallowed. "Yeah, that's crazy," he replied. They heard somebody knocking at the door, so Troy went to go get it. As he opened the door, he saw two big police officers and police cars surrounding his block.

"Are you Troy?" they asked.

"Yes," he replied nervously.

"Can I come in your house to look around?"

"Why?" he answered.

"I don't know if you know this, but there was a drive-by at 12 a.m. last night, and we gathered some people who said that a black BMW was driving in this neighborhood around 12:30 a.m. So we wanted to look in your house for anything that might help solve the case."

"Okay," Troy said.

As they looked around the house, they stopped at Troy's door and opened it. Troy remembered that he'd left the gun under his blue jacket on his bed. His heart dropped as the police stepped in and looked around. They saw his blue jacket. One officer walked up to it and picked it up. The gun wasn't there. The officer checked Troy's pockets, and nothing was there either. They ended the search and thanked them for their help.

Troy closed the door. His mom cleared her throat. "You have a lot of explaining to do," she said, with the gun hanging out of her purse.

* * *

My belief is that you always have a choice, because you control yourself. Don't get pressured into doing something you don't want to do. See, Troy's life wasn't bad at all, but he let his surroundings take control of him. He had a good life. He was one of the smartest kids in the class. But what messed him up was society. He wanted to fit in with the so-called "cool people."

I believe that you always have a choice, and Troy did too, but his choice wasn't the right one. As kids, our dreams were to go to the NFL by getting drafted to play for the 49ers. But instead of going down the road to success, he went down the road society pushed him toward, which got him in a hole that he couldn't climb out of. When I hear stories like this, I think to myself, *Why act like something I'm not and get caught up in a hole like that?* I don't ever want to be what I'm not, so I've promised to always be truthful with myself. I have a choice.

The reason I go by this belief is that I have had to deal with racial profiling all my life. One day I was walking home and this lady was in front of me. She just paused and stared at me like I wasn't even human. I felt alienated. When she looked at me, I knew what she was thinking about me. She thought I was non-educated, a dropout. She looked at me like I was going to rob her or something. She rudely judged me as what I was not.

I thought to myself, *This is just another obstacle.* I just had to continue walking on, because I had a choice to entertain her ignorance or be smart about it and keep moving. Man, I have been racially profiled for all my life. Every time it happens, it doesn't bother me, it just reflects off of me. My belief is so powerful that it gives me strength to absorb their negative energy and turn it into nothing. I have a choice to not entertain the stupidity of ignorant people.

A lot of people have followed this belief, such as Martin Luther King Jr., Malcolm X, and Rosa Parks. I respect those people who stood up, because they had a choice to be quiet or stand up, to get up from their seat or to stand their ground, to have a nightmare or to have a dream. And I respect those people who fight for our nation to make sure we are safe and don't get attacked by other countries; I respect everybody who strives for their goals. If I didn't believe in this I would be torn apart, because I wouldn't have the strength that I have today.

Some people don't share this belief, but it would do them good at times because it might help them push themselves to the limit.

Sometimes the easy way out is the bad way, and you just need that one push to get the job done. Sometimes instead of begging for something, you have to get it out of the dirt.

For example, once when I had a football game, I sprained one of my ankles and my other one was already sprained. I went to the doctor that night and he told me that I shouldn't play in the game the next day. But I thought to myself, *I'm not going to let a doctor tell me about my abilities.* That night, my dad and I had a long talk about whether I should play. He told me, "It's your choice to play or not. You'll risk both of your ankles." But I still said yes, I would play.

In that game, I scored three touchdowns, made fifteen tackles, and had five force fumbles. By making a choice to risk sacrificing my ankles, I had one of my best games in my football career. At the end, the result was promising because I got a reward from my team for having the best game that season. I made the choice not to take the easy way out, and to keep working toward my dreams of becoming an NFL player.

Sian Adelina Laing was born in San Francisco and has lived there her whole life. She is fourteen years old and has a little sister who is ten. Sian likes roller coasters and heights because she loves the feeling of flying. She likes the saying, "Whatever floats your boat" and tries to live by this ideal. Sian enjoys gymnastics and hanging out with her friends.

HOW A SCARECROW AND A VIDEO CHANGED MY IDEAS OF BEAUTY FOREVER

BY SIAN ADELINA LAING

Imagine this. You and your friend are given some money to buy some nail polish. However, you both have to agree on one color. You see a shiny black, but your friend insists on fluorescent orange. You both argue over which color is better, but neither of you can agree on one color because you both believe that your choice is best. This is a perfect example of beauty being in the eye of the beholder.

I believe that beauty is in the eye of the beholder. I was always a relatively open-minded person, thanks to the guidance of my parents and their words of wisdom about how everybody is unique. However, I didn't think about it that much until the day I discovered a video on YouTube that helped to embed this belief in my brain forever.

It was a sunny afternoon on June 30, 2014. I was stretched out like a lazy cat on my bed, scrolling through suggested videos from BuzzFeed. I had seen almost every video until I scrolled up one more. There it was, the video that would change my perception of the world forever: "Beauty Standards around the World." This particular video caught my eye because, being a teenage girl, of course beauty would intrigue me. I eagerly touched the cold, shiny screen and waited for the video to play. The video had an unusual and exciting premise. A woman sent an unaltered photo of herself to Photoshop experts around the world with the instructions, "Make me beautiful." The next part of the video blew my mind. The pictures that were sent back to her varied so much in so many ways. Some Photoshop experts had darkened her skin, changed her eye color, even changed her clothing! When the video ended I was dumbfounded. Never before had I seen so many different opinions! Even in the comments people were giving their feedback on what they considered beautiful and what they didn't. This video gave me a sense that I had been enlightened. It hit me like a bolt of lightning. Stunned, I realized that arguments over beauty are pointless! Because there are so many different ideas of what is beautiful, insulting another country's or person's idea of beauty is childish. In the end, beauty comes down to individual and cultural taste. I'm glad that after seeing that video, I have a better understanding of what "beauty is in the eye of the beholder" means.

Another incident, much earlier, started my belief that beauty is in the eye of the beholder. It was a cold and cloudy day in November 2008. Brooke, my teacher, stood tall and graceful like a queen at the head of my third-grade classroom. Brooke informed us that the Fall Fair was coming up in a couple of weeks and our class was entering the scarecrow competition. At my school, Creative Arts Charter School, the scarecrow competition was a competition where each class had to build a scarecrow from scratch and attempt to win first place. Brooke asked who wanted to work on the scarecrow and my hand immediately shot up, as did many of my peers'. We got started immediately. I had a vivid image of the scarecrow in my mind. It had overall jeans, a plaid shirt, a straw hat, and a pitchfork. I thought it was perfect and an ideal scarecrow. However, before I could even open my mouth to pitch my idea to my classmates, a dozen other voices cut me off. " I want to make the scarecrow from *The Wizard of Oz*!" "I want to make a zombie scarecrow!" Voices were coming in from all sides. Then the shouts changed from ideas for a scarecrow to accusations of how stupid the other ideas were. "No! That's a stupid idea!" "Our scarecrow will be a joke if we do that!" The chaos continued, and I soon found myself joining in. I remember standing up and shouting, "All of these ideas will make our project look nothing like a scarecrow! We should use my idea!" My classmates looked at me for a couple of seconds and then continued to fight. The rest of the day flew by, and we got nothing done.

I walked home that foggy day with a scowl on my face. I kept thinking that if the class had just used my idea, we would have had a perfect and beautiful scarecrow that was sure to win the first place ribbon. I brooded over this thought for quite a while, until I had a grand revelation: *Why do we have to have a perfect scarecrow?* Being only eight years of age, this idea blew my mind. New ideas and plans for the scarecrow flooded my brain. I couldn't wait to share them with my peers the next day. I was the first person at my table, ready to discuss the plans for our scarecrow. This day started out the same as the previous one. My classmates argued and yelled about whose idea we should use. However, this time I was prepared. After I finally got the group quiet, I shared my idea that we would all use a small part of our own ideas to put on the scarecrow. It took a while, but my classmates warmed up to the idea and eventually loved it.

We got started on the scarecrow. I brought in a pair of old jeans, the person who wanted to make a snowman scarecrow brought in cotton balls to add a snowy effect, and the person who wanted to make a scarecrow from *The Wizard of Oz* brought a straw hat. Many other people brought bits and pieces of clothing and inanimate objects that embodied their vision for our class scarecrow. When we finally finished, our scarecrow looked amazing. It had claws, a zombie face, snowy feet, jeans, a straw hat, and sparkly shoes. Even though it did have a bunch of completely unrelated objects and clothing placed on it, we were proud of our work. Everybody loved it, and apparently the judges did too. We won first for creativity and received much praise for our interesting idea. This experience taught me that everybody has their own idea of perfection or what we call "ideal." Every one of my classmates had a different opinion on how we should portray our scarecrow, and every single one of them thought that theirs was the best. But I think we all learned that beauty is in the eye of the beholder, because we all learned to respect each other's opinion.

One person who respects and shares my belief is my mother, Mina Laing. As a young adult, she worked in the fashion industry and witnessed many incidents where girls who were not skeletons or who did not have flawless skin were turned down as models in a horrific manner. In fact, she told me that one of her dear friends often worked as a model. However, she struggled with her weight and constant acne breakouts. One time when my mother accompanied her friend to got to a photoshoot, the woman in charge came up to my mother's friend and screamed, "Oh my God, look at you! You are hideous! Lose all of that weight and get rid of that acne if you ever want to model for us again!" My mom told me that her friend cried for days. Just because my mother's friend didn't fit into the woman's idea of beauty, she was shunned. This experience led my mom to teach my sister and me that we should not worry

"If people struggling with body image and fashion designers alike could understand this belief, we could fix and prevent so many issues many girls and boys face today."

about our weights and that we are beautiful just the way we are. These are words of wisdom that I keep with me even today. This shows that this belief could be a key in fixing many problems our society faces. For example, if people struggling with body image and fashion designers alike could understand this belief, we could fix and prevent so many issues many girls and boys face today.

The fashion industry is a cruel world. Everybody is striving to create a perfect image to sell their brand or what they consider to be beautiful. The CEO of Abercrombie and Fitch is a prime example of how when people don't respect other people's ideas of beauty, or any idea other than their own, disaster strikes. In an interview with *Salon* magazine, the popular clothing store Abercrombie and Fitch's CEO, Mike Jeffries, stated, "We hire good-looking people in our stores. Because good-looking people attract other good-looking people, and we want to market to cool, good-looking people. We don't market to anyone other than that." This single statement caused outrage from many different teens, their parents, and the media. Abercrombie and Fitch is known for having gorgeous but provocative models who wear very little clothing. By saying that Abercrombie and Fitch only hires good looking people to work for them because they want to market to good-looking or "beautiful" people, they are saying that anyone that does not look like their employees or models should not be considered beautiful or even be able to wear the same clothing as "beautiful" people. By saying this, Mike Jeffries is implying that "ugly" people should be treated as lower-class citizens.

Even though many people, especially media and the fashion industry in our day and age, are very intolerant of different body types and beauty, something is being done about it. Slowly but surely, things are changing. For example, the theme of big and curvy girls being

SIAN ADELINA LAING

beautiful is prominent in many forms of media, such as the song "All About That Bass" by Meghan Trainor. Many lyrics in this song argue that bigger girls and girls with curves are beautiful. The line "Yeah, it's pretty clear, I ain't no size 2, but I can shake it, shake it, like I'm supposed to do," perfectly describes this point. It also shows that our society is realizing that there is a problem with only appealing to one idea of beauty or only having one idea of beauty. In addition to this, plus-size models are all pioneers in having more than one idea of beauty portrayed in media. Lane Bryant first began selling clothing under the category "For the Stout Woman" in the 1920s. In the 1950s, the store actually put plus-size models into her catalogs! This made Lane Bryant one of the earliest pioneers of adding a more varied image of beauty in media and fashion. The fashion industry is still evolving! MiLK modeling agency recently signed the biggest plus-size model in history. At five foot five and a size twenty-two, Tess Holliday, also known as Tess Munster, is opening new doors for models.

This belief is so important in so many ways. If everybody believed this, many problems people in our society face could be solved! Self-esteem and body-image issues could be prevented or have new ways of being dealt with. Personally, if I saw more diverse models and actresses in media I would worry a lot less about how much food I consume on Thanksgiving, or how much exercise I would have to perform to work off that cheeseburger I just ate. The reality is, if everybody understood that beauty is in the eye of the beholder, everybody would be a lot happier. Back to the nail polish incident: you and your friend should respect each other's opinions because beauty is in the eye of the beholder.

Jefferson Mach is a fourteen-year-old freshman at Mission High School who came to San Francisco from Guatemala City in 2011. When he can, he enjoys going home to Guatemala City to enjoy the taqueria-style foods, like burritos. He also enjoys playing soccer in his backyard with his agile two-year-old brother. He later hopes to attend a good university and possibly venture into business in the future.

OH MAN! NOT AGAIN!

BY JEFFERSON MACH

Have you ever been in a situation where you're afraid of saying the truth and you feel like lying? Well, some people get away with it, but others don't, and instead they make a problem even bigger. Lying can be a good thing. For example, if you're on the streets and a strange person gets next to you and asks you if you're alone, you'll say no, that's your mom right there, but you actually choose a random woman. But lying can be a bad thing, because if you lie to someone, even to a family member, then they will get mad. You'll have to pay for the problem; not with money, but with really bad consequences. Throughout my life, my experiences have made me believe that lying can get you involved in bigger problems.

When I was in middle school, I told my friend, "Lies can hurt you, and when somebody catches you lying, you will end up with bigger consequences." But my friend said, "I don't care what you say and I don't believe it, because every time I lie, I get away with it." Two weeks later, he came up to me and said, "You were right; lying can get you into bigger consequences. I lied about my homework and my parents caught me and took away my laptop for two weeks." This relates to me because I used to lie too, before I believed in my belief.

A year or two earlier, it was a sunny day, a nice day to go to school. I got to school safely and went directly to my classroom. I was sitting at my desk, waiting for the teacher to come. Ten minutes passed. Everyone in the classroom started to jump around as if they had won the lottery. I could hear a lot of kids screaming and books falling off the tables. When I saw how fun it was, I joined them and started to play around, too. Out of nowhere, the teacher came in the room. I got a pencil and threw it, hitting her on her head. She was really angry and yelled, "Who threw this pencil?!" Nobody answered. I thought I got away with it, but then the principal called me and said, "Jefferson Mach, please report to the principal's office now." I was so scared as I went to his office and opened the door. When I looked at the principal, my face was red like a tomato. I looked at my leg and it was shaking like an earthquake. The principal asked me, "Did you throw the pencil?" I said, "No." Then the principal showed me the video from the security camera, and we saw that I had thrown it and lied. The principal said, "You lied to me and now you will face consequences. I don't want to suspend you from this school, so I'll give you another chance." I was so glad he did not suspend me from school, but he did call my parents and they took away my phone for a week. From that moment on, I stopped lying because saying the truth is the better choice.

One day, I had a soccer game to play at Crocker Park. My mom told me to get ready to leave the house in ten minutes. I didn't really listen to my mom, so instead I got my soccer bag and went to the couch to play some video games. When my mom said she was ready, we left the house and went directly to the soccer field. Once we got there, my mom told me to change fast because I had to play in five minutes. I opened my bag and found a huge surprise. I had forgotten my soccer shoes at home and only brought my socks and shin guards. When my mom came back and asked me if I was ready, I had to decide if I should tell her the truth or lie. I told her the truth

JEFFERSON MACH

and said, "I forgot my soccer shoes at home." She was a little angry, but she just told me that I wouldn't play that day. If I had not told her the truth, maybe she wouldn't have taken me to the next soccer game for not being responsible. I feel like saying the truth was a better choice than lying.

In my life I always try to remember that when you lie, if someone catches you, instead of being happy and glad you will be mad and sad. Saying the truth is a good way to keep a friendship or to make your life better. And I will still believe this, even if other people don't, no matter what happens in my life.

Rosemary Higgins is a San Francisco native who enjoys her afternoons perusing Tumblr. She secretly wishes she could shoot spaghetti out of her fingers. She's also a unicorn. Some parts of this bio aren't exactly true—but which ones?

NO, GO AWAY.

BY ROSEMARY HIGGINS

My belief is that people should learn to unapologetically say no. The first time I heard of this belief, I was scrolling through Tumblr. It got my attention mostly because I was confused about what it meant. The first thought that came to mind was, *How could someone feel sorry for saying no?* I guess I was taking it too literally, because the more I thought about it, the more it made sense. More often than not, people say, "No, I'm sorry," and stuff like that. This applies to the quote because it is an example of literally apologizing for saying no. The quote also applies to just wanting to say sorry, or feeling guilty when you don't give someone what they want and want to take it back because you feel bad.

I think this is a good belief to keep in mind because it's a good way to stand up for yourself. If you don't do that, people will walk all over you and take advantage of how you feel guilty or whatever. When you learn to stand up for yourself, it helps you a lot. You start standing up for yourself in other things. Your confidence will probably go up and you can become more vocal and not be afraid of being heard. Also, when you start feeling more confident, the guilt from saying no will slowly fade away, and soon you will ruthlessly crush the skulls of your enemies and triumphantly bathe in their blood.

One example of this belief in action (no skull-crushing involved) is in a cartoon called *Foster's Home for Imaginary Friends*. Will was the imaginary friend of a child who loved basketball, and was created to talk and basically play basketball with him. He was as tall as a basketball pole, super skinny, and bright red. Also, Will is really, really nice and understanding, like a therapist. Will was put into the foster home after he lost his arm and they thought he couldn't play basketball anymore. Coco is a goofy-looking bird that is part crashed airplane and part palm tree. She can only say "Coco" and lays eggs with weird items inside—things you normally would not find in an egg. Will and Coco are also best friends. In one episode, Will was having trouble saying no to Coco. Coco would ask for things and make ridiculous requests, and Will just went with it. He felt like if he said no, Coco wouldn't want to be friends, and he was getting frustrated from saying yes to everything. Finally, when he said no, he felt super relieved. Although Coco didn't like being told no, mostly because she was so used to getting what she wanted from Will, she understood Will's need to stand up for himself and was eventually cool with it.

Standing up for myself is difficult because I take into consideration the other person's feelings and well-being more than I do my own. I feel like if I say no, the person will get angry or threaten me somehow. For example, there was one time when one of my friends wanted me to do her Spanish homework. Usually I would do it for her and it was no problem, except this time, I really didn't want to do anything, much less someone else's homework. I was also afraid that she would stop talking to me if I didn't do it. I didn't want her to feel bad for asking me, so instead of saying no I just made up a ton of excuses. I said my phone was glitching and that I couldn't see the pictures she sent me, and that my phone died so when it turned back on it deleted our conversation. I thought she would just give up sending it to me and just finish it herself. That did not happen. Eventually, I just felt really bad and so I just did it. I wish I had kept my belief in mind at that time because she's a really good friend of mine, and I'm sure that had I just said, "I'm really not in the mood to do someone else's homework right now," she would have understood.

I think that a lot of people face the same kind of anxiety when thinking about saying no, especially if it's to a friend. You don't really consider how if this person was really your friend, they wouldn't make you feel obligated to do favors for them. Something that you can think about is what your reaction would be if you had a friend who said no to you. You would probably feel a little disappointed, but it probably wouldn't bug you that much, and not enough to break off the friendship. An example of this is when I didn't have lunch one time, so I asked my friend for food. My friend said no because she was hungry, so I just shrugged it off.

It's kind of weird talking about this, and telling people why this is a good belief to have, because I am really bad at following my own belief. I try to, and I think about it a lot. I definitely still need to work on it. But that's okay. I know that gaining confidence and being comfortable with standing up for yourself takes a lot of work and patience.

Anthony McBride lives in San Francisco with his father and is a freshman at Mission High School. In his free time, he enjoys playing basketball. He plays center on the Mission High JV team. His favorite subject is math.

WINNING IN THE END

BY ANTHONY McBRIDE

As a basketball player in middle school, I came to understand that quitters never win and winners never quit. I rolled my ankle during practice once when going over a play. The throbbing pain was the most I had felt in my lifetime. My coach allowed me to stop practicing. When I got home to check my ankle, it was red like a tomato and painfully swollen. I couldn't walk for a month. When my ankle healed, I didn't feel like going back to playing basketball for a while, because I was afraid of getting injured again. My dad let me take a few days off after my ankle healed. When a week had passed, he wanted me to go back.

We argued because I still didn't want to go back. Then he told me that quitters never win, but I didn't believe him.

"I don't want to go," I told him.

"You have to finish what you started," he said gently. I disagreed with him and decided to go back to school, but not to basketball.

Another person who helped me understand my belief is my sister. When she was playing basketball, her team played against girls who were taller. When the game started, it seemed like my sister's team had already given up. They looked scared and they moved like snails. It looked like everyone on her team didn't want to play,

"When the game started, it seemed like my sister's team had already given up. They looked scared and they moved like snails. It looked like everyone on her team didn't want to play, but my sister kept being positive and trying to keep her teammates' spirits high."

but my sister kept being positive and trying to keep her teammates' spirits high. She kept encouraging her team to play harder, and when the time expired, they were able to win by a point. That showed me that quitters don't win. I started to realize that belief more, but I was still a quitter.

Then the time came when I hurt my ankle, and I refused to go to basketball practice because I still thought I was going to get injured. A teammate came to me in the hallway and told me that if I didn't show up to practice, I would be off the team. The coach had told the team that I was close to being kicked off.

During class that day, I had time to think about playing basketball or having more time for hanging out with friends. When I was thinking about that, I also thought about what my dad said to me about not quitting and finishing what I started. That helped me choose basketball. I decided to go back to practice, and the team was able to make it to the playoffs. Even though the other team knocked us off, this helped me become a better basketball player, and that felt good.

Joan Landers is a fourteen-year-old ninth grader, born and raised in San Francisco. She is half El Salvadorian and goes to visit every couple of years to fill up on pupusas. She claims that "Netflix is life" and "If you don't make me read, I'll read on my own." Her other favorite hobbies include eating, sleeping, and playing soccer.

STAND UP FOR YOURSELF

BY JOAN LANDERS

I didn't always put myself in the mind set of "Life is too short to care about what other people think, so stand up for what you know is right." But when I started thinking like that, everything changed.

It began in sixth grade when people would tell me all these things that they had heard about me. At first I was confused and didn't really comprehend the situation. When I first realized I was getting harassed, I felt my heart drop. I knew this was a common thing, but I never thought that it would happen to me. I would get mean text messages saying that I'm a "skinny pencil." They were also the ones who wrote cruel words on my locker. Finally there came a time when the bullying wasn't such a secret anymore because it became so bad that it was noticeable. My friends began noticing before anyone else did, but still nothing changed. During that time, the bullying intensified and I began getting threats in my Facebook messages.

It was a dry day and I was at Beacon, my after-school program. I began getting anonymous texts from an unknown number calling me a really awful name. It was sent multiple times. I couldn't take it anymore, so I told Valerie at the Beacon program. Her face was in complete shock—it might have turned as red as her hair for a split second. Valerie doesn't tolerate any form of bullying.

She helped me out by responding to the anonymous texter from my phone telling them who she was. She also threatened to file a police report about the harassment. What she did for me made me feel better about the situation, but that still didn't make me feel safer. So I went to the police department and they suggested I take this to the Board of Education.

Soon after my grandma and I went to the Board of Education to request a transfer, but they suggested that we have a meeting with the school principal, vice principal, and a police officer to see if it was worth transferring. The school decided that my excuse to transfer wasn't "sufficient." That was the moment I decided to speak up for what I knew was wrong and change it, but my request was denied. This cold day I was extremely hurt, but it caused me to change my mind set to believe that life is too short to care what others think, so stand up for what you believe.

The following Monday, I returned to school and the air felt thick with the ideas from the previous week. I got pats on my back from teachers and staff saying, "Glad to see you back." This made me feel even more cautious about the situation. I didn't feel comfortable with people knowing about my problem, and it made my heart drop knowing that the teachers had a conversation about it. I already knew that the police had visited the girls' houses and spoke to them about what happened to me. That honestly made me feel uneasy about everything. I didn't know how the girls would handle the situation and react toward it. Deep down in my head, I was scared because I didn't know if it would make the situation worse or solve anything. But, surprisingly, everything cleared up and I never heard from them again. Standing up for myself despite what other people think made life easier for me.

The Black Lives Matter movement is something very current that relates to my belief. I think that there has to be some type of emotion involved in their protesting that causes the activists to speak up for what they know is right. The activists know that they are fighting against a system. There is a possibility that the outcome could be dangerous. There are many chances for people to look down on their actions, but the protesters decide to overlook that negativity because in reality, there will always be someone who doesn't like your actions. But then you might come across a person who shares your belief and may decide to join your fight. Their movement is an inspiration that shows that if you advocate for what you know is right, despite what others may think, a change could happen.

A change occurred for me after I spoke up for what I knew was right. During that time, I still was scared about what could happen, but I decided to put my fears behind me and move on with life. The Black Lives Matter movement has shown that when you stand up for what you know is right, despite opposition, the outcome will most likely be positive.

Declan Clark was born in San Francisco and moved to Mazatlan, Mexico when he was seven. He lived there for four years. His most vivid memory of that time is of watching the World Cup in the living room. He has a fraternal twin brother named Riley and has played soccer since he was three years old. He plays soccer for Mission High and is proud of the team's impressive record. He says that soccer is his life but he doesn't like the running part.

MAKING THE RUN

BY DECLAN CLARK

It was the first day of soccer practice; I was nervous, but hopeful. I had heard from many people about how physically demanding the Mission High School soccer team practices were, but I still wanted to join. On this warm fall day, the grass was a deep green on the school's soccer field and the sky was a gorgeous light blue. Practice started with standard warm-ups such as stretching, running, and passing drills. I noticed that most of the upperclassmen were very relaxed, as if they were used to this. As practice wore on, I started to realize how physically challenging it all was, but I hadn't seen anything yet. At the end of practice it was time for sprints. We sprinted the length of the field back and forth five times. My whole body felt like Jell-O. That's when I realized: *This is what I will have to go through to make progress.* I was frightened because that meant I was going to have to go through a lot more pain and exhaustion. Could I do it?

Each practice was a new challenge, and I was up for all of them. I wanted nothing more than to stay on the team, and it was clear as day that this was what it was going to take. Over the rest of the season, I developed the following belief: in order to succeed, you have to want it as much as you want to breathe when you are drowning. That has to be your level of dedication. Sure, it may be hard; it will be the most difficult part of your life, but when you finally get it, all of the pain, sweat, and tears will be worth it.

There were lots of times when I had to look to my belief for strength to continue. For example, on the hottest day of the year, we had a game. It was against a not a very skilled team, so almost everyone was in good spirits. We all went into the gym to change into our white home uniforms, which we did before every game. As we were changing, our coach, a former marine, came out and yelled that the team we were supposed to play had forfeited. At first everyone was happy, but then he said we were going to have to get the exercise that we would have gotten from the game. We started the "practice" with hundred yard sprints back and forth. After a while, they felt like miles. Next we raced the football team, and whoever lost had to do fifty up-downs. I had to will myself not to quit. I made it through another hour of intense training in ninety-degree weather, thinking about how important my belief is to me.

The sensation of really physically working hard is a bit debilitating. The muscles in my legs burn, my heart pounds in my chest, my stomach churns, and my breath shortens. Over all of that, however, is the sensation of progress, which tells you that you are getting better, and this is what tells me to keep going. I know that this is what anyone who has succeeded has felt.

My belief has been challenged by my parents several times. One time in the car, my mom told me, "You have to have a backup plan for when—I mean, if—this whole soccer thing doesn't work out."

Her words were like a bunch of needles in my eye. This was probably one of the worst things to say to your son while driving him to his soccer game. In the backseat, I proceeded to ignore her, because, frankly, I was really insulted by this. I've heard this countless times from both of my parents, but I have learned to just shrug it off. Of course I know that she's right, but I'd like not to think that way. I'd rather be hopeful for the future instead of waiting for my dream to not work out. If you want success as much as my belief states, then two people criticizing it should not shake your dedication.

I think my belief is important because it helps motivate people to do better. Not everyone has the willpower to go out every day and give everything they have to try to get success. I think that if more people were exposed to my belief, they would be out pursuing their dreams and putting it all on the line to find success. Of course, I know that there is much more to success than willpower. There are tons of variables that have to be accounted for, such as quality of living, opportunities, financial stability, and so on. I'm not saying that only wealthy people with lots of spare time can be successful. What I am saying is that anyone can be successful, but not everyone has the same opportunities to do so. Willpower may get you to where you need to go to compete at the highest level, but that does not mean that you will win. However, even if you don't win, the fact that you put everything on the line to get where you are will land you further in life than if you had not tried. This makes me a bit hopeful, because even if I don't find success doing something I love, all of my hard work will not go unrewarded. Even though I didn't win, at least I made it this far.

Brando Garcia is a quiet, relaxed fifteen-year-old. He grew up in San Francisco's Mission District but has family all over North America. He speaks both English and Spanish and loves movies and math.

SPEAK UP

BY BRANDO GARCIA

We all have experienced being asked a question and not wanting to speak up because we fear our voices not being heard.

I was and sometimes still am a quiet person. When I was younger, I barely talked because I never wanted to speak up about anything. I guess I was just born a quiet person, because I don't talk much at all. I still don't know why, but I only speak up about certain things. I'm pretty self-sufficient when it comes to things about me, but otherwise I still don't talk about stuff I need. I don't ask people for anything because I don't want to bother people with anything, even if I know them really well.

For example, one time I asked my brother to go buy me something from the store, because I knew he was going out. He said no, he didn't want to, and he didn't hear me out. I wondered why he didn't want to; I thought it was him just being mean, which made me confused because he is usually nice. Then I realized that he just wasn't listening to me. I was debating in my mind whether I should talk or not. I finally made up my mind that I wasn't going to say anything anymore, so I didn't. I couldn't help but feel somewhat disappointed, because I wish that I had spoken up and said something back to him. But I'm a quiet person and didn't want to say anything, so I went and back in my room and played games.

So that's why I believe that people don't want to listen to anyone about whatever it is they are talking about. I always thought people just didn't care about anything anyone has to say, but I have since realized we all have a voice and should be heard.

We should always hear someone out, even if we disagree with them. You might not agree on everything, but maybe you will agree on certain things. You could have a certain opinion about what they're talking about or you may change your opinion based on what they're saying. They have a voice too, and it should be heard, even if you don't like what they're talking about.

For example, my school had a dress code and a majority of the school didn't like the uniform policy. A group of students decided to ask the teachers if they could change it in any way, and some of the teachers there didn't think they should change it. Some teachers, however, were willing to listen to what the students were saying. They didn't agree with everything the students had to say, but they still both agreed that students shouldn't have to wear it all the time. The group of students and the teachers came to a somewhat-agreement; not on all things, but on the fact that students shouldn't have to wear uniforms all the time.

The teachers heard out the students, even though some teachers didn't want to change the dress code. They decided to listen to them, and this is why I also think we should always listen to people about what they have to say. The teachers listening to students about the dress code, even though the teachers are in control, proves everyone has a voice that should be heard.

As a result, I've started to realize that if I speak up, I could change certain things. I have the same or different opinion, even if no one agrees with me, because my voice can be heard. You can always learn new things through what people are talking about if you hear them out.

"They have a voice too, and it should be heard, even if you don't like what they're talking about."

Giovanni Aguilar is fifteen years old and was born and raised in San Francisco. He dreams of visiting Rome. He enjoys playing football and baseball and is a fan of the Giants and 49ers. He is into rap and hip-hop. He plays a lot of video games. He hopes to attend college at Ohio State, Texas A&M, Oregon, UCLA, or UC Berkeley.

WORK HARD, PLAY HARD

BY GIOVANNI AGUILAR

I like to have fun, so that is why I work hard. The harder I work at school, the more I enjoy and appreciate my free time. This belief started when I was just messing up in my life, and I was seeing homeless people living on the street. I told myself, *I don't want to be like that.* I want to be someone in life and I have my family telling me to not mess up in school and to work hard. Life is short and time goes by quickly so it is up to me to make my life successful.

One rainy dark day, I was waiting for the 27 bus in downtown San Francisco when I saw a homeless man. The homeless man looked dirty and he wore a red-and-brown jacket that was ripped and stinky. His pants were all ripped and he was wearing a San Francisco 49ers cap. He had some Nike shoes that were old and dirty. He was drinking a Budweiser. When I saw the man, I felt bad, so I gave him like five dollars to buy something to eat or drink, even though I thought he would go buy more beer. He came up to me and he asked, "What is your name?" I told him my name was Giovanni. He said he came from Reno and he began to tell me his life story. He told me when he was a little boy he had an abusive dad and he said that his dad would always beat up on him and his mother. He said he was so sad and scared that he would just go with his friends and use drugs and drink alcohol. He said he went to school and got in trouble too much and that he wishes he would have finished school and applied himself. He said he wished he didn't use drugs and alcohol. He told me, "Kid, you look like a nice kid. Don't be like me."

When I heard his story, it made me start to believe that I needed to do my hard work first and then relax later after I finished my work. My mom and grandma always tell me, "Pay now, play later," and I try to take their advice. They tell me life is hard now, so do what you have to do and don't mess up in school. My hard work now will pay off later. Hard work pays off in small ways and large ways.

I remember a time when I worked really hard and did well in school. I had raised my GPA by a lot by spending more time doing homework, paying attention in class, and staying after school to do my work. My mom took me to L.A. because I achieved my higher GPA. This vacation was an example of how hard work pays off, and now it was time to play!

We traveled there with my cousins and uncles and aunts and my brother. We went to Disneyland and Knott's Berry Farm. It was Halloween. When I was at Disneyland, I enjoyed walking during the night on Main Street. It looked beautiful, with nice white lights, and everything looked Victorian and antique. It smelled really good, like buttery popcorn, churros, and ice cream. I asked my mom if she would buy me an ice cream. I asked for chocolate peanut butter fudge; it tasted amazing and I really enjoyed that day. After we ate ice cream, we got in line for our first ride. We waited for thirty minutes or an hour, but I was excited so time went by fast. My favorite ride at Disneyland is either Tower of Terror or Space Mountain.

Space Mountain is so fun and exciting. First you get into your seat and start moving up into a tunnel, and then you corkscrew through outer space. A man counts down to launch, "10, 9, 8, 7, 6, 5, 4,

3, 2, 1...GO!" and then you go really fast and navigate stars and meteors and it is exhilarating. It is so fast. I sat next to my cousin, and we both had fun. It felt like a long time, but before I knew it, we were back where we started. When the security seat belt unlocked, I stepped out onto the platform and felt dizzy. I like to go on rides late in the night, too.

Next we went to Haunted Mansion, where you get into a black circle with two people. I was with my cousin and the ghost host started talking about the ghost and how haunted the mansion is and how it was time to try to find a way to escape the Haunted Mansion. We went around and saw floating candles and knights in shining armor moving by themselves, and a lady with a head in a globe. Then we entered into the dining room and kitchen as the ghosts were dancing around us and singing. We exited the Haunted Mansion and saw a cemetery all around us. Then the ride finished and a lady's voice said, "Please don't forget to come back, and bring your death certificate with you when you come."

After that, I decided to go to the Pirates of the Caribbean ride. Here, I got inside a boat and put on my seat belt. We were going slowly through the dark and we began to see alligators in the water and then we encountered a man playing the guitar. Then a pirate appeared and we went into a tunnel, and we entered into an area where pirates and ships were all grouped together. As we got close to a battle between two ships, the water started to boil with cannon fire, and pirates were fighting with swords. A pirate was looking hard for Captain Jack Sparrow, and they were singing, "Yo ho, yo ho, it's a pirate's life for me!" and they continued to battle with gun fire. Then I saw a pirate sleeping with two pigs near him. Then Jack Sparrow appeared and he was singing; he was wearing a gold crown and was adorned in gold jewelry. Then the ride was over and we got back on the street.

Then we went to California Adventure, and I rode on Tower of Terror. It's a big, old antique hotel building. We walked inside and there were old antiques, like a doll sitting on a chair, and we went into an elevator. The voice of the dude from *The Twilight Zone* came through the screen. We saw a family that got electrocuted and we dropped down, and then up and down five times. My arm was hurting because it was so abrupt, but it was so fun. I have been on this ride so many times; once I went on the ride six times in one day.

Next, we went to Knott's Berry Farm on Halloween to see my cousin's dance crew, Academy of Villains. For this night only, it is called Knott's Scary Farm. My cousin and her boyfriend own Academy of Villains, and this was a big performance. My cousin dances and her boyfriend both choreographs and dances. Academy of Villains danced with Elvira, Mistress of the Dark. I went twice to see her in two different years. One year she was dressed like a clown, and this year she was dressed like a zombie. Everyone was wearing a tuxedo with zombie face paint. My cousin's boyfriend was an evil clown with an orange and black tux. He had a zombie face, too. There were a lot of dancers, and they did a really good job. I felt enchanted by the dancing; I was excited and amazed. The music was dubstep. Elvira sang. It was surreal.

After the show, we went to the haunted mazes area. The mazes are really cool and scary. I was there with my cousins and we were getting chased by monsters in the mazes. They would run and scream, but I wouldn't. What was cool was that my little brother went inside the maze by himself, so I thought that was funny. One maze was called Pinocchio's Revenge, another was called Black Magic. I liked all of the mazes. I never felt lost in the mazes; mostly I was excited and a little bit scared. I hate it when the actors pop out and startle you. When I got out of the maze, I felt an adrenaline rush. I felt relieved to finally see the end of the maze.

GIOVANNI AGUILAR

There is a good place to eat at Knott's Berry Farms and it's called Carne Asada Fries. The fries were crispy and amazing and the steak was really juicy. We all loved the day.

When I went back to my hotel, I was really tired, so I lay down on a nice bed. It was as comfortable as sheep's wool. Before I went to sleep, I told myself, "Thank God I did really good in school because now I am really enjoying myself. Hard work really does pay off!" I was really excited for the next day.

You can at least play a little bit when you have your free time. The "play" part is important because sometimes hard work can stress you out, and you could get depressed because all you have to do is work and stress. It's also important to play so you can be with your family and have good communication with others. Being with your friends helps you enjoy yourself and get relief from all that hard work and stress. Sometimes I have to remind myself to believe in my belief because sometimes I think that the hard work does not pay off. Then I start not caring and I just start playing too much. When this happens, this is what I do: I think in my head, *When I'm bored I should finish my work so that when I have free time, I can play so much because I don't have any work to do.*

My life has been really good ever since I started to work hard and enjoy the payoff. I wouldn't be in the ninth grade if I'd never believed in myself. I want to succeed in my life, so I work hard. I think if the world believed that working hard pays off, there wouldn't be so much homelessness and everyone would have money and a house to live in and a job and they would be happy. Sometimes this is not easy, and a job might not pay you enough while you're doing a lot of work. Even if you don't like your job, you have to work hard now so that you can be free after and enjoy life. Lots of people suffer, but if they work hard they could have a better future and a happy life.

"You can at least play a little bit when you have your free time. The 'play' part is important because sometimes hard work can stress you out, and you could get depressed because all you have to do is work and stress."

I also think that people should remember to enjoy playing too, and find a balance between work and play.

Back to the homeless man that I was talking about in the beginning. I think about the stuff he told me, that he should have worked hard but he didn't. He told me, "Don't end up like me." I always think about what the homeless man told me. Always work hard and you get your free time to enjoy! Sometimes it's good to believe in paying now and playing later. The world would have peace and be cleaner if people would not just be in the street, making it dirty. If people believe that hard work pays off, and they "pay now, play later," they will enjoy life.

Humberto Zatarain was born in Mexico and came to the United States with his family before he could chew. While he's a skinny guy, Humberto loves double-doubles at In-N-Out. An ambitious fourteen-year-old, his sights are set on attending Juilliard and the University of California at Berkeley. Humberto likes pop ballads and emotional male voices, like Sam Smith's and Bruno Mars'. Hopefully someday he will get up onstage himself!

MUSIC SAVED ME

BY HUMBERTO ZATARAIN

I was around thirteen at the time when I was thinking of self-harm. I fell into depression. Everything, like just sitting in class or riding on the bus, felt like I was the only one there. The people in the courtyard were ghosts passing by me. Unwelcome thoughts would creep into my mind at night. I could feel the cold, silvery knife in my dreams, as if it were pushing against my skin. I would wake up in the middle of the night. I tried not to think about it.

Today is the greatest day I've ever known. The Smashing Pumpkins wrote the song "Today" for one of the band members. He was thinking about suicide at the time, so the band wrote the song. After school my sister would play Rock Band on her PSP. She would play with the volume so loud it sounded like the band was in my house. I would hear the songs over and over. That's when I first heard the Smashing Pumpkins: they had exciting drums and shocking, soft, delicate guitar melodies. On the weekends I could play the game. Sometimes I would sing the songs aloud to myself. Most of the songs were energizing. *Live right now / yeah, just be yourself.* Others were sad. *My angel wings / Were bruised and restrained.* But singing always felt great.

One of my friends that I used to talk to found out that I was depressed. She asked me, "What's wrong?" I told her I felt like a fish stuck in the middle of the ocean with no one near me. She told me she's been where I've been, she said it wasn't fun, and it truly wasn't. Then she

"The song goes, *Today is the greatest day I've ever known. It's* probably because he is still alive."

asked if I was self-harming. I said, "No, but I'm thinking about it." She told me it's not worth hurting yourself to feel that something isn't there. That made me not self-harm. The song goes, *Today is the greatest day I've ever known.* It's probably because he is still alive.

Before music, I hated school. I didn't know what I wanted to be and I didn't see the point in doing my homework. I started to sing and listen to music to cope with the situation. After a while I thought less about my loneliness. I was more content. I did fall into depression again, but the nightmares were gone. I just sing and my problems fade away. I feel alone and at peace.

I believe that feeling happy is a choice. It's not always an easy choice. It's easy to feel indifferent when you're not doing what you love. But once you're doing it, every choice is easy.

Singing helped me release my fears emotionally instead of physically. Now I dream of attending Juilliard University. I know thousands of people send in audition tapes and only a handful make it to auditions. Even then, only six percent are accepted. But I believe I can do it. I want to pursue my dream of music. It's a passionate way of life. Music helps you through tough times. I'm still a little bit afraid to sing in front of people, but when I do, I know I'll be helping other people through tough times. We all need something to care about.

If you're suffering from depression or thinking about self-harm, check out the website sfsuicide.org or call the National Suicide Prevention Lifeline, 1-800-273-TALK. It's better to get help sooner rather than later. It might be tough, but it's worth it. You don't have to suffer alone. I wish I had known about these things at the time. Don't be ashamed to get help if you're struggling.

Tamerah Grady was born in San Francisco on the day after the Fourth of July nearly fifteen years ago. She loves pizza and scary movies. Friends say she is always laughing or being goofy. If she could have a superpower, she would choose to read minds. As of now, she's an expert reader of faces.

BREAKING A GENERATIONAL CURSE

BY TAMERAH GRADY

A generational curse is when something is repeated in your family. You did it, your children do it, your grandkids do it, and their kids will do it. In my family, my mom didn't graduate high school because she had my brother at sixteen, and my brother didn't graduate high school because he got in trouble his senior year and dropped out. In my family, the generational curse is not graduating. Even though my family's generational curse is not graduating high school, I believe I have the choice to make my own footsteps to graduate high school and college. By staying focused on work, doing my best, and not giving up, I know I can break the curse.

There are always little things that get in the way, like an obstacle course. On the show *Wipeout*, they have different activities that block you from getting to the end. Sometimes you try to jump on the ball, but the balls are slippery and you end up slipping and falling and you have to go back to the starting point. Some everyday obstacles in life are getting up, catching the bus, going to class, doing your work, paying attention, and doing your homework. If you fall off track, you won't reach your goal because it is hard to get back on track. If you fall for one thing, it messes up everything.

Everyone faces these obstacles, but if you have a generational curse, these obstacles are harder to overcome. You put a lot of pressure on yourself to break the curse. This pressure isn't always a bad thing, but it can be exhausting. I have been staying on track by doing my work, turning in assignments, paying attention in class, and asking for help. Sometimes I just don't have the motivation to want to do my work and pay attention, but I force myself to pay attention because I have to get through it to break the generational curse. I get myself together, step outside to take a moment to myself, and take a breather to get ready to go back in class to get what is about to hit me.

My mother didn't graduate high school because she wasn't really focused on school like she was supposed to be. She ended up having my brother at sixteen and dropping out of high school so she could take care of my brother. Taking care of a child can be hard and trying to go to school at the same time was too much for her to handle. What stopped her was she didn't have the support that she needed to succeed. She regrets not finishing school and wishes she could go back to ninth grade and take school seriously. She always tells me this or talks about it when I am around so that I know how important it is to finish school in order to have a productive life. My brother didn't graduate high school because he got in a lot of trouble in the middle of his senior year and was suspended. When he was able to come back to school, he was so far behind it was to hard for him to catch up. He made the choice to drop out because he didn't think he could do it; he lost faith to the point where he gave up.

I have faced a lot of obstacles as well. Going into freshman year of high school, I wasn't myself. There were too many things going on. My house had flooded due to a broken pipe. My mom and I were living in and out of hotels just outside of the city. There were bedbugs in the hotel. My mom was bitten by a bedbug and had to

TAMERAH GRADY

go to the hospital. We slept in our house even though there were still blowers there to dry out the house and we couldn't breathe. Then there was an earthquake. It was crazy. One thing happens and everything can fall apart.

All of this stress overwhelmed me. I couldn't sleep. I did not want to start at a new school. I did whatever I could to get things off of my mind. I cheered, I spent time alone in the shower, I listened to music. Eventually, my mood started to change. I still had a little bit of negative energy, but I overcame it by doing the right things for me. I had a somewhat difficult time adjusting to my new school, Mission High School, but I got comfortable and kept going.

Even though there continue to be stresses, I won't give up. For example, during finals week, I was really worried about my geometry and physics tests. I went to an organization called College Track for help and asked for a personal tutor to help me in those subjects, but they never were able to get me a tutor. I got frustrated because I was trying to get help, but no one could help me. I felt so annoyed that I decided to give up. For two days, I didn't care. I would go to class and sit there not knowing what I was doing. I paid attention but didn't understand what the teachers were saying. The teachers were trying to help students but their systems weren't working for me. For example, in geometry class, we work in groups. Groups are supposed to work together and help each other. In my group, some people knew how to do the problems but they didn't know how to explain it well. I was sitting in my group, feeling lost. I asked for help from my group members and they tried to explain things, but it only made me more confused.

After school that day, I was in the car with my mom, driving home. We were talking and there were a lot of things going on at once. My grandma was in the hospital, my auntie was stressed trying to take care of my grandma, I was undergoing a study for my own health problems, and I knew I had to do well on my final exams in order to pass the class. I looked at my mom from the backseat with an irritated face and said, "I'm overwhelmed and all these things are going on." I realized I was focused on all of these problems and had developed a pattern of negative thoughts. Everything started to come out and I had a breakdown. I started crying, quietly sobbing and feeling even more irritated that my mom was telling me that she had told me not to start off running by doing all of these extra activities. When we got home, I was still frustrated. I didn't want to study for my finals but something told me I could do it. I pulled out my notes and studied, studied, studied. I wouldn't give up because I knew I had to believe in myself to break the curse.

The next day, I went to physics class with my one page of notes, which I had reviewed as my study guide before taking the test. My teacher handed out the first page of the test. I looked at it and realized I had been stressed about nothing. My notes were good. They matched the test. Then the teacher handed out the second page of the test. I skimmed it and felt it was a little bit harder than the first one. I looked at my friend who sits across from me and asked if we could switch notes, which is something we were allowed to do in this class. She said, "Sure." Her notes matched the second part of the test the way that mine had matched the first. I was excited. I knew I had done well on the test.

Next came geometry. I felt nervous because I didn't think I was going to pass the test. I was scared to be working on my own and not in a group. My teacher passed out the four page test. I looked at it and decided it was going to be hard, but I decided to try my best. If I got something wrong, I told myself at least I tried by studying. I didn't complete every answer. When I got to a question that

I didn't know, I left it blank and came back to it at the end. When the bell rang, I hadn't finished. There were four questions I still needed to solve. I didn't panic. I knew I could still pass even if I wasn't able to solve those problems. I made a decision to believe that I could pass the exams, and I did. I felt like my generational curse was testing me, to either give up or believe in myself. I chose to believe in myself because I want to break the curse and graduate.

My name is Tamerah Grady and I attend Mission High School. I wanted to tell you about my story because I want people to see that generational curses can make a person feel like giving up when really, there is always a choice. Even if you have a generational curse on your back, like me, the choice is yours to give in or fight back. When someone is in a fight and they're exchanging hurtful words, they either have the option to walk away or throw the punch. When someone is angry and they have a gun, they have the option either to pull the trigger and shoot or just walk away and leave the situation alone. If you want to break a generational curse, you have to know that the choice is yours.

IT'S OURS

STORIES OF COMMUNITY

Joseph Lake is from Hunters Point in San Francisco. He is fifteen years old and the youngest of three siblings. He is full of humorous and insightful life advice, like "if every pork chop was perfect, we wouldn't have hot dogs." He hopes to travel to Jamaica someday. When he grows up, Joseph dreams of playing in the NFL, practicing sports medicine, or being a veterinarian. He also wants to own a red-nose pit bull.

WHAT IT MEANS TO BE A TRUE FRIEND

BY JOSEPH LAKE

"If he can't break bread, he fake." This line was rapped by L'A Capone, a Chicago rapper murdered at the age of seventeen as he was coming out of the studio. The first time I heard this song, I was at home on a rainy day with my older brother Mike. We were listening to another Chicago rapper named Lil Durk on my PS3. The way my PS3 is set up is that if I'm on YouTube listening to a song, it plays the next suggested song after the song I'm listening to. After Lil Durk, the L'A Capone song came on and the beat slapped, so my brother and I said, "Keep it on," even though any other time we would change the song. Then, in the middle of the L'A Capone song, he said, *If he can't break bread he fake / I had one more buck on my plate, it was me and bro / we was in the store and both of us got fifty cent cake.* I turned to my brother and said, "Did you hear what he just said?" He said, "Yeah, I know." Before I even heard the song I was breaking bread, meaning sharing the last of my money, or some of my money. I was splitting it in half with a friend because they have no money. If I didn't break bread I wouldn't be a true friend, meaning I would be a fake friend.

An example of breaking bread was when Malik, Justin, and I went to the taco truck in Valencia Gardens. Justin's dad had just won the lottery, so he gave him 300 dollars. Justin treated himself to a burrito, treated me to a burrito, and treated Malik to a taco. This was the ultimate breaking bread because he spent so much money on us. Another time Malik and I were in the store and I only had one phony, crinkled-up dollar in my pocket. I broke bread with Malik and we each got fifty-cent honey buns. It doesn't matter how much money you spend breaking bread, what matters is that you practice "bro-osity"—a sacrifice to make you and your bros happy. Breaking bread is a lot more than just buying food for your friends. It's knowing that, when you're in need, your friend will be there. It's knowing your friends will have your back. And most importantly, it's being a true friend.

Some people don't break bread, which makes them fake friends. One time I was on the 22 bus and this boy I used to be cool with asked me to come to the store with him. I asked him if he was going to buy me something because I had no money. He said yes, so I went to the store with him. It was a long day and I had already spent my money earlier, so I was hungry. The store was super far away—really just two blocks away, but I was hungry so it felt farther. We got to the store and he got a fruit punch fifty-cent soda and a honey bun. I was like, "Where is my honey bun?" Then he pulled out a ten-dollar bill, gave it to the cashier, got his change back, and walked out. As we walked back to our destination, he just ate in my face. My stomach was hurting, so to this day we are no longer cool. And since he didn't break bread, he's a fake friend.

Not everyone knows about breaking bread but anyone can learn, just like Marcellus did. One day I was at the Boys and Girls Club and it was boring so Marcellus said, "Let's go to the store."

I said, "I don't have any money."

Then he said, "I'll buy you something."

I said, "Okay."

But when we got to the store, he said, "I'm not buying you anything." Then I thought, *If he can't break bread, he fake.* At that moment I guess it clicked in his head, and he bought me something. Then a couple days later he didn't have any money, and I bought him something. Ever since that day we've been bros.

If the whole world broke bread with other people it would be a better place. There would be less killing, stealing, fighting, and arguments. People who are doing those things maybe do them because they feel like no one has their back. They feel empty inside, like a discarded soda can. But when someone breaks bread for you, you feel like someone cares and it gives you hope. If you're sharing money, there would be no one to fight because you're being kind and breaking bread. There would be fewer killings because some killings are over money. If someone is buying you something, there's no need to kill or steal because someone is buying those things for you and being a true friend. Also, if you're the one giving or sharing your money and preventing these killings and robberies it makes you a better person inside because you're caring for other people and not just yourself.

One time, when I was at a party, my friends knew this guy but I didn't know him. When we all went to the store in the middle of the party, he came with us. We had already spent our money before the party, so we all had like three or two dollars left. When we got there, he asked Malik and Justin to buy him something, but they said no. Then I was like, "I got you." So I gave him fifty cents to get himself something. We've been cool ever since then. About two weeks later, I saw him on the bus with like three other dudes; I guess they wanted to rob me. But he was like, "No don't do it, that's my bro." So they didn't do it. I'm so glad I gave him fifty cents that day, because you never know when fifty cents will save your life.

Brenda Aceves, age fourteen, is a San Francisco native with roots in Mexico and Guatemala. Her favorite food is pozole, and she is afraid of clowns. She has three sisters, and if she had one superpower, it would be to visit places no one else can—maybe somewhere like heaven.

HOW TO STOP MOTHERS FROM CRYING

BY BRENDA ACEVES

Have you ever lost a close family member or a close friend due to a senseless act of violence? My belief that "change starts with you" relates to history; consider, for example, Martin Luther King Jr. There was change because he was brave enough to stand up and fight for what he believed in. Because he was one of the first to stand up for what he believed in and got people's attention by having a powerful voice, he had people support him and he made a change. Another example is Rosa Parks. She was sick and tired that the African American community had to sit in the back of the bus, so she sat in the front, even though she wasn't allowed to. She made a change by standing up for what she believed in. If she never sat in the front, it might still be that way. If you want change, all you have to do is stand up for what you believe in.

My friend was murdered on September 2, 2014, by a former classmate we went to school with. My friend was only fourteen years old, and he got his life taken away over hate and jealousy. Losing a friend made me feel like the ugly duckling; I was sad and alone. Losing a close friend motivated me to start doing movements against violence. One reason why I believe there should be no violence, especially violence toward innocent victims, is because no family should go through a horrible pain like we went through. It's pretty sad how I can't even watch the news anymore because any time I watch the news, there is always another case of an innocent person dying. Sometimes it's over something they're not even involved in. It makes me really sad when I hear stories like that, because I know the pain they feel and it makes me feel like I'm going through that pain all over again.

On a sunny yet windy Saturday two days before Martin Luther King Jr.'s birthday, January 17, I attended a march for victims who were murdered by police brutality and senseless street violence. The march started at St. Anthony's Church. From St. Anthony's Church we marched to 24th and Mission, which is where there are a lot of tourists and people coming and going like the waves in the ocean. When we were marching I heard everyone's loud and powerful voice. I could smell bacon-wrapped hot dogs sizzling on a cart. I could feel my hands aching from holding the banner for too long. We stopped there and made a little circle; in the circle two families talked about how they lost their loved one. They talked about how they wanted violence to stop. Hearing their stories made me feel numb, as if I was getting shot myself.

We started to walk to 16th St. and Mission, and at 16th we did another circle. My friend's auntie talked about how he died and how he was as a person. Listening about how he got murdered made me feel like I was living the horrible dream again. After his family talked about him, a lady told her story about how she recently lost her son. After she talked about the loss of her son, we went to Dolores Church and had a mass for all of the souls that have been lost due to violence.

BRENDA ACEVES

Attending the march made me feel like our voices were being heard by everyone. The power of our pain made me feel like our voices weren't being ignored.

In my opinion, I think we should all come together to fight for change to stop senseless violence. Two ways I can do this are by bringing together people who have been through the same thing, and by touching people by telling them how my friend passed away. Marches are effective because they're a group of people who went through the same thing you did, and they understand where you're coming from. You can't do it by yourself. For example, if I did it by myself, it wouldn't be as powerful; you always need someone by your side to support you. A world without violence wouldn't have as many depressed mothers shedding hurt tears over the loss of their children. Another way the world would look is peaceful and happy.

I believe if we all come together and try to do something to stop violence, we can stop the violence toward innocent victims. It all starts with one person, and I want to try to be the person to stop senseless violence.

Gerardo Lopez was born in Mexico and moved to San Francisco when he was two years old. He enjoys drawing and playing soccer. His favorite food is pepperoni pizza.

A VERY MISLED PERSON

BY GERARDO LOPEZ

I wasn't always respectful and grateful toward my mom and dad. I used to make assumptions about them. Now I believe that respecting and being grateful for your parents and not making assumptions about them is a way you can get a better future, a good career, and a stronger relationship. Seeing them as people with problems too can help you better understand them and yourself. It is a way life can get easier.

One day, I was at home. It was a bright day. All I heard were birds singing and cars passing by. Every time I saw my mom, she didn't talk to me or listen to me. She was always on her phone and cooking at the same time. She was also cleaning our room and the kitchen. I was mad. I was also bored. I thought about going to the park to play some soccer and to forget about what was going on. I did not ask permission that day, so I was afraid that I was going to get into trouble. I came home early; my mom didn't say anything, so I predicted that she hadn't noticed. Later on that day, both my brothers came up to me and asked me if I knew what was going on with my mom. I didn't answer, because I also had that question in my mind. I was really confused that day.

At night, I played my PlayStation4. All I heard were the sounds of my controller and gunshots coming from the video game. It was as boring as sitting in class, but it was a good way to think. I couldn't sleep because I was worried all night.

The next day, I woke up and heard my dad speak to my mom. I was so curious that I felt like going up to them and asking them what was going on. But instead I stood very quietly and listened. I didn't hear much besides "bills, bills, bills." I thought that maybe they had been busy all day the day before.

Later, I went up to my mom and asked her what happened. She just told me she was confused. She didn't know where to pay the bills because it was never explained to her. She was new to the United States, so she didn't know anything about bills. I wonder why my dad never told her about the bills and where to pay them. I realized she was going through a lot of conflict and stress. This is when I learned that making assumptions about your parents can make life more difficult. From then on, I chose not to make assumptions and to always respect them.

Before I respected my parents, I did many bad things. I wasn't thinking wisely. I mostly thought that my parents didn't really care about me. When my parents took me to the mall, there was a sandwich store. It seemed like a liquor store because of the snacks they sold and how small it was. I was starving, as if I hadn't eaten for a week, but I was scared to ask my dad for a sandwich because he would always say no. I grabbed a sandwich from the takeaway fridge when the workers were busy and ran off. When I was enjoying my ham-and-cheese sandwich at a table, my dad came up and asked me where I got it from. I didn't answer truthfully because I was afraid, so I said, "I found ten dollars on the floor." He believed me. Later on, one of the workers came up to me and told me I had to pay for it in front of my dad. My dad just looked at me with an angry and disturbed face. I was so scared, but thankfully my dad just paid.

GERARDO LOPEZ

He didn't really talk to me the day after that happened. He was as silent as the inside of a library.

The next day he came up to me and told me to never steal again. I told him I was starving and thought that he didn't care about me. He said that if I was hungry, I could've just asked him for money to buy a sandwich instead of doing something unnecessary. Basically, I was always wrong about my dad. I thought he never cared about me, but then I realized he actually did. Not respecting your parents can get you to do things you don't expect yourself to do just to get attention, like stealing a sandwich. If I never learned to respect them, many things would be hard for me since they help me a lot, especially in becoming a responsible adult and student. I would have a totally different personality. I would be a troublemaker or a very misled person without them.

In conclusion, believing that you should respect your parents, and understanding that they're people with problems too, can help your relationship with them and also make you a respectful person. I started believing that my parents are always with me, always helping me and making sure I'm okay, even if sometimes it doesn't seem like it. I'm thankful for having parents who really care about me. There are people that say they're lucky to have a parent who lets them do whatever they want, but in my opinion, those parents don't have a heart for their child. I'm glad I have parents who are always there for me and help me when I'm having problems. They're everything to me.

Sarai Gonzalez is a fourteen-year-old student. She was born and raised in San Francisco and her friends often come to her for honest and nicely phrased feedback on their selfies. Her favorite word is her own name, she loves eating pozole, and she quickly picks up dance moves to any style of music. A few years back, her first-grade teacher provided the striking insight that writing should be naturally conversational and ultimately convincing. She keeps this in mind whenever she writes, and finds writing liberating.

THE MISSING FATHER

BY SARAI GONZALEZ

On a foggy day in San Francisco, I find myself looking at my dad's pictures, wondering where he is and what he's doing. At age two, my father left for Mexico and I grew up without him. But I believe that good things come from bad things.

I was jealous of the kids and their dads dropping them off at school while I was with my stepdad. I felt distant from him even though he had always been present, since my first memory. I rejected his kindness without letting him in. When my stepdad bought me ice cream, I arrogantly replied, "I don't want anything that comes from you." When my mom sat down to discuss my behavior, I disobeyed even more. I remember her saying, "This happens to a lot of kids, you're not the only one. You have to be brave."

Peep peep! My alarm went off. I refused to accept that my mom was about to get married. It was the morning of May 10, 2009, a day I had wished would never come. Stylists arrived and all I did was look at them angrily. They showed my mom her wedding dress.

My face turned beet red and I was tempted to throw my pomegranate juice all over the dress. But turning toward my mom, I was shocked to see how beautiful she looked. I smiled at her, but remembering again why she looked so stunning made me upset. My mom asked me if she looked nice, but all I did was say "Mhm" and walk away.

I was the worst ring bearer, with my head down the whole ceremony. When I finally stood up to give my mom and stepdad the rings, I started crying.

By the end of the night I dropped my sadness and shed tears of joy. My mom's contagious and beautiful smile made me realize her happiness was the only thing I wanted, whether it was with my real father or not. I congratulated both my mom and stepdad and apologized for thinking only about myself and not them.

After the wedding, there was a total transformation of my relationship with my stepdad. I opened up with him and accepted his hugs, his "Good job," the rides he gave me to school. I realized that he was the head of the family and he cared about us. Before, I avoided him by staying in my room, but after, the house opened up and my door was never shut. My real dad's absence was less hurtful and I was able to accept my stepdad's invitations to spend time with him.

* * *

It was the morning of May 30, 2010; it was cloudy and dark. My alarm went off, but when I woke up, I was home alone. I slowly opened the squeaky door of my room and walked around the house yelling "Mom?" but no one responded. I was worried because my mom was nine months pregnant and I didn't know where she and my stepdad were. Suddenly, I saw my sister standing in the kitchen. I gasped and said, "Where is Mom?" but she didn't know either so she called my mom. Unfortunately, she didn't pick up.

That same day I had a big Brazilian parade performance, where I was going to dance. I got to 25th and Harrison, where the performance began. Seeing all the colorful costumes, face paints, crazy hairstyles, music, kids, and float cars started to cheer me up a bit. When we started dancing, I was still anxious. The smell of the churros, doughnuts, and the combination of other sweet smells hit my face, and my tummy started to growl, but nothing stopped me from dancing. Four hours in and two blocks away from the finale, I was looking for my sister among the crowd but she didn't seem to appear. I waited at 17th and South Van Ness for my sister for thirty minutes and when I finally saw her running toward me, her eyes were as shiny as a pot of diamonds. When I asked what had happened, she gave me the surprising and great news that my mom had been in the hospital because my baby brother was finally born, which made me feel excited and very happy to finally be an older sister.

My family dealt with my selfish attitude by hoping for me to finally accept my stepdad. His persistence indicated his desire to be part of the family. I took myself out of the situation and recognized the mutual happiness he and my mom brought each other. I believe we can take the troubles life gives us and, with the right attitude, turn them into positive journeys.

Beatrice Griffin was born in San Francisco and loves working with theater tech, costumes, and sewing. She likes reading comic books—especially manga. She is learning Chinese and really enjoys listening to punk rock and emo music.

THE DIFFICULTY OF LOVE

BY BEATRICE GRIFFIN

Many people say that you have to love yourself before you love others, but what most people don't realize is that it's easier said than done. Loving yourself can be a difficult process to do alone. I think that people don't realize how hard it can be for so many people to live in the world with all its inequality and anger without doubting themselves.

Before I started believing my belief, the idea of self-love meant nothing to me. I didn't object to the idea, but I couldn't think of any circumstances where it's hard to love yourself. I started hearing about how a person has to love themselves before they can love another person and I didn't really agree. I really started believing that if you don't love yourself, the love of another can make your self-worth greater. And I had seen posts on Tumblr about how when someone else loves you and you love them, they can make you feel better and help you find out more things that you like about yourself.

People who influenced me into believing that it's not necessary to love yourself first to love others were my teachers, who taught me about mental illness such as depression, anxiety, OCD, and low self-esteem. Also, when I went on the Internet, I would come across things about abusive relationships that involve addiction and mental illness. In those places, it's hard to find a way to get out. In a situation like that it can be hard to love yourself because you aren't getting love from your partner. Learning about mental illness really showed me and gave me an idea about how hard self-love can be in places where you don't feel loved. After that, I really started to open my eyes about these problems, the effects they have on the mind, and the way mental illness impacts self-love.

If you love yourself, you can always be more positive about yourself, but I find it is important for others to help. Even if you don't love yourself, if you love someone else, the person you love can still help you realize how amazing you are. For example, I have a friend with some personal problems, and whenever I tell them how great they are, they thank me and tell me, "I'm glad that I have a friend like you that cares so much," or something similar. This just proves that good friends can make you realize how amazing you are.

I have doubted this a bit. For example, a while ago I was reading about how people who are depressed laugh the loudest and try to make others laugh, too. Because of that I thought that my belief that self-love is not the most important kind of love meant less and didn't apply as much as I thought. Then I realized that those people who laugh the loudest need someone to laugh with, too. I realized that even if they seem happy, they still need somebody else to help.

For example, Robin Williams had many problems, such as alcoholism and depression. Although this is reflected in his comedy, the fact that he was in comedy sort of proves my point about how depression can lead comedians to trying to make people happy and laugh because they don't want people to go through what they do. Robin Williams was a comedian and actor who made people laugh and tried to get them to smile because he knew how it was to feel lousy.

In general, it's vital to have someone help you and love you, even if it isn't in any sort of romantic way. Even if you don't have any romantic intent, it is still important to have someone by you who has affection for you or just wants to be close to you. I know someone who has depression and some other mental illness, and we often send each other messages over the Internet. I always try to make them feel better about themselves when I send them messages because they are so kind and deserve to feel appreciated. They are always very kind-hearted when they write. Sometimes they bring themselves down; because of that, I try to make them feel better, because they are really quite amazing. I found with this friendship that we connected in a different way compared to others. Instead of meeting at school or having a friend of a friend, we kind of solely met by chance. The fact is that we both found each other interesting enough to message each other over the Internet. When we started talking, we both were very kind to each other and we still are, but now we know more about each other and understand what the other needs. This relationship has boosted my belief that help from another person can boost someone's self-esteem by seeing it in action because I can read their happiness when they reply.

If I didn't believe that if you don't love yourself, a love of another can make your self-worth feel greater, I wouldn't see how it helps others. I wouldn't notice how when I compliment someone who is very shy or has low self-esteem, that they take it so well and find happiness as a result of the love that I show them. When you compliment someone who isn't used to getting compliments, they almost shine with happiness. But because I believe this, I do notice these little things, which can really make a difference. I also think if I didn't believe this, I would not find as much meaning in compliments when they're given to me. I would struggle more and reject most people. I think I would keep to myself and not do much.

"I think that people don't realize how hard it can be for so many people to live in the world with all its inequality and anger without doubting themselves."

Self-love might be unhealthy compared to a healthy relationship with a family member, lover, or friend. The media's obsession with perfection makes self-love seem like something it's not. This is why it's important to have someone guide you and teach you how to love, because not everyone knows how.

I think if someone has troubled thoughts and self-esteem issues as well or even just needs support, they should consider taking my belief into mind. For example, when you're down and you are hurt badly, it's hard to get up on your own without someone helping you and caring. The people around you can determine the way you feel about yourself.

I think everyone should believe that it's important to have the love of others to feel adored, because it's amazing to feel loved by someone. When you have loving people around you, you can really feel marvelous, while if you have negative people around you, it can get you down. I think if people did consider this, a lot more people wouldn't be struggling with accepting themselves, because it is very hard to do alone. In the end, self-love and acceptance can be a struggle for a lot of people, but with help from a loved one, it's much easier to find self-love.

I'Jah Pratt was born in San Francisco and has five brothers and sisters, including an identical twin. All of them are experienced athletes. I'Jah's grandmother is from Louisiana, and he still has relatives there. I'Jah is quiet until he gets on the basketball court with his teammates.

I'M LUCKY TO HAVE THIS FAMILY

BY I'JAH PRATT

There are six kids in my family. Shakiyla is my oldest sister, and she's twenty-four. Herman is twenty. I'm fourteen. My twin brother U'Jah is also fourteen, and my brother and sister Jahzara and Jahfari are both eight. We live in Hunters Point, San Francisco, in a green-yellow-and-white house. My family is very important to me, and not just my immediate family, but my extended family too. I have a lot of cousins and I see them pretty often. Family is important because we have fun together and we help each other out.

U'Jah is my twin brother, but he is also like a friend to me. I think of him as a real friend because he shares stuff with me. For example, U'Jah will usually share his food with me. The other day, U'Jah went to the corner store after school with some of our friends. I didn't want to go so I decided to stay at school. I was hanging out by the gym when they all got back and I saw my brother carrying a bag of Hot Cheetos. I was hungry and those chips looked good. When U'Jah walked up to me, I asked him if I could get some chips. He held out his bag like it wasn't a big deal, and I grabbed a handful. Some of my friends share their food with each other, but not always. Some people are so hungry they won't share things. The way U'Jah shares things with me makes me realize he has my back.

Another thing U'Jah does is he will always come to support me in sports. He will come and watch me play if we don't play on the same team, like last year when he played varsity football and I played JV football. On our last game of the season, he came to watch me play because he loves watching me play. Before the game, I was getting dressed and U'Jah came by the locker room. He walked up to me and told me to play hard. I said, "Okay," and gave him a high five. During the game, I saw my brother in the crowd. He was sitting in the stands with our friends who were also on varsity, watching the game. It made me feel good to see my brother at my game because he came to watch me.

Just because U'Jah and I are brothers doesn't mean we always get along. Sometimes we get into fights. Recently me and U'Jah got in a fight because I was messing with him. We were play-fighting but then I accidentally hit him in the side. He got serious and punched me and then I punched him back. He threw me across the living room; then I got up and jumped on him. He threw me down and punched me five times. After the fight, we calmed down and started playing NBA2K again. This shows that brothers love each other, even when they fight.

Another person who helps me is my older brother Herman. Herman is in college and is tall with long hair, like my dad. He is twenty years old and wears a size fourteen shoe. He loves playing basketball and video games. One moment that shows that he is a good brother is that he drives me to practice sometimes. He comes and supports me at my basketball game or football, too. He takes me to go work out with him. Herman lets us play his game, but we have to ask him, and he took me and U'Jah to go see *The Maze Runner*. That movie, was a good movie. It was a Saturday morning. Herman said, "Lets go." We said, "Where are we going?"

He was going to the movie. After the movies, we took a long ride home. When we got home, we played the game.

It is important to look up to people, because then you will know where your life is going and the person you look up to is setting a good example for you and you will follow his footsteps. If you don't look up to somebody, your life will be boring. My younger brother and sister look up to me like I look up to Herman. They look up to me because I do stuff for them, like buy them candy and make their food. It makes me feel good that my little brother and sister look up to me, because it means I'm a good influence on them. Having my brother and sister look up to me means that I have to be good in school for them. This gives me a little motivation because I think of them when things get hard at school. For example, I used to not like to do my work in class. One time, I had to do a lab report for physics. It was too hard because I had to write all about what we had learned in class. A part of me wanted to give up, but I didn't. I didn't give up because I had to finish so I could turn it in and get a good grade. Getting a good grade was important to me because I wanted my brother and sister to know that grades are important. If they see me getting good grades, they are more likely to get good grades, too.

Life without my brothers would be boring. I wouldn't have anyone to hang out with or anyone to play sports with. My brothers also help me out. They make sure I do my homework and they help me do the right thing. It's not just my brothers who help; my parents do, too. My dad is a great father. He pushes me to do my work at school and my dad coaches me in sports. My mom makes sure that we have our stuff clean in the house before we leave the house and makes sure we are doing well in school, too.

Rosa Cruz is an independent, well-organized fourteen-year-old from San Francisco. She comes from a big family and she enjoys listening to music, exploring outdoors, and cooking pasta. English is her best subject and she enjoys writing because it is therapeutic for her.

A WORLD WITH GRATITUDE

BY ROSA CRUZ

When I was ten years old, my dad came back into my life. It was on a weekend around 11 a.m. when my mom took me to Silver Terrace Park. I remember wearing my elegant burgundy dress. As I was standing in the park, it was as cold as a December morning. I kept asking my mom, "Is it him?" I was so anxious. When I finally saw him, he walked up to me and it was the craziest feeling in the world. I was excited but felt weird, like I was meeting a stranger. He wanted to catch up with my life and me. He stayed here for a week or two, and then after those two weeks he left my life again, this time forever. When my dad left, I felt really sad and confused. After a while, I felt hopeful again because I had my mom and a great life with her. His leaving made me realize how grateful I was for my mom and the life she had given me. It made me see that I just needed her. I realized that it wasn't just about my mom; I began to believe that everyone should be grateful for what they have in life. I am glad that my belief started at a young age, when I was just ten years old.

Before I had this experience, I hadn't focused on what I had. I always wanted more—more clothes, electronics, or food. I used to take everything for granted, like the things my mom would do for me. For example, she provides a roof above my head and she cooks food for me every night. A meal she cooks for me that I love is spaghetti with cut-up sausages. When I was at home and we wouldn't finish dinner, I would throw away the leftover food. I felt it didn't matter because it was just extra food and I didn't realize that so many people don't have access to food. Now I'm grateful for every meal I have and every day that I get to wake up.

Realizing how grateful I was for my mom made me grateful for everything in life. Sometimes with the little things I forget to be grateful. I take things for granted, because meals or clothes seem like little things. Even the smallest things are important; for example, a homeless person would probably be thankful for a warm blanket. If you're grateful for what you have already, you'll be happy and want to give more to those who have less than you. You would be more fulfilled because you would feel glad for what you already have. When I forget to have gratitude, my sisters usually remind me of how much we have. In my daily life I am reminded of how much I have when I see others who have less than me. I feel thankful for the privilege of sleeping in a warm bed and being able to receive an education.

If you're walking down the street and you see a homeless person, you might not think that a dollar or two or maybe some food or blankets would help them. You're on your way to eat something and go home to a warm bed. Anyone with less than you might be grateful for the smallest things. There is a homeless man in my neighborhood; he is friendly to all of us. He has this brown pit bull that he is really close to who protects him and all of his belongings. In return, the homeless man feeds the dog, so he's pretty chunky. One day, my sisters and I were going to get breakfast, and we saw him. We figured we should bring him some breakfast, too. When we gave it to him, all he could say was, "Thank you, God bless you." He was as happy as a toddler getting a new toy on Christmas. Everyone in the neighborhood would bring him food or supply him with blankets. When someone is grateful, they are delighted with what they have, so they want others to be happy, too.

I feel that everyone should have gratitude, because when people are stingy and greedy, their personality looks ugly. They have a lot but want even more. Also, if you're really greedy and selfish, you take everything you have for granted. Imagine if the world believed or practiced my belief; our world would look so caring and less awful. Everyone would want to give more to others and be grateful for the small things they have. If more people would start believing this belief, they would want to be more caring to others. If people started caring for each other, it would make everyone else more peaceful.

Basically, I'm thankful because I've learned that you don't need more to be happy in life. I've learned this by experiencing my dad leaving and seeing the poverty in my city. These experiences taught me that if you're not grateful and you take everything for granted, it can all slip away and you can lose everything you treasured. Everyone should be grateful for what they have because there are people who have less than them. I will practice my gratitude by not asking for more than what I have or need, but by helping those who have less than me. I believe everyone should be grateful for what they have, because if you are, you'll be fulfilled and want to give more to those who have less than you.

Adam Sabatino was born in San Francisco. Some of his favorite things to do are playing baseball and Ping-Pong, drawing, watching TV, chess, and board games with his family. Super-competitive family fun includes Stratego, Monopoly, and Risk. He also plays varsity baseball and soccer for Mission High School. To keep up his strength and stamina, he eats his favorite foods, tortellini and spaghetti with meatballs.

ALWAYS ASK HOW YOU CAN HELP

BY ADAM SABATINO

My friends and I were on a train going home when we heard a woman yelling for help at the back. We turned to see what was going on when we saw a woman holding a kid's hand. He was stuck in the doorway and had gotten separated from his mom. The woman helping them sounded scared at first, and then angry that the driver wouldn't stop the train. After hearing the woman's cry for help, we ran over to see what we could do and we told the driver to stop. He wouldn't listen and just kept driving. Then I looked around and saw that no one other than the screaming woman wanted to get involved. I was surprised that these people thought it wasn't their responsibility to help. At the next train stop the woman helping took the little kid off the train and back to his mother. This made me feel that the people who didn't help didn't care. I think it's important to care because if it were me, I would want someone to help and care about me.

This reminds me of something I just watched in health class. We were watching clips of people doing random acts of kindness. One of the stories I saw was about a police officer bought a pair of shoes for a homeless man. This stood out to me because the officer wasn't looking for any fame and wasn't looking for a reward. He was on patrol and he saw a man out in the cold, freezing his feet off, so he decided to go to the Skechers shoe store and buy the man shoes and socks. The homeless man was so happy and thanked the officer. When the officer wasn't looking, his admiring partner snapped a picture and sent it to the station. A few days later the chief of police gave him a medal. I think he deserved the medal because he did the act out of the kindness of his heart. This story reflects my values. It's important to do something from your heart to help other people, whether you know them or not.

I think it's also important to do this with your own family. One time, on a cold and rainy day, I was sitting on the couch watching TV when I noticed that our kitchen was really dirty. I got up to get some cereal and I couldn't find a spot to set the bowl down. There were piles of dishes and food on every counter. I thought for a second and told myself this was unacceptable. I decided that the kitchen wasn't going to get clean by itself and I needed to clean it. So I started cleaning all the dishes, clearing off the counters, and putting everything in its place. Then I took a sponge and wiped all of the surfaces free of the food bits and dirt. When I was done, the kitchen looked better than new. When my parents got home, they were so happy my mom hugged me and asked why I cleaned up. I said I just wanted to help out. I felt good inside because I had done something good without being told.

There have also been times when I didn't want to help, like when my dad asked me to clean the basement and I didn't feel that was my responsibility. I felt that if he wanted it done, then he could have done it himself. There are times I feel angry, like I'm going to have to do a lot of work and it's going to take a lot of time out of my day. Other times, like when my dad was cleaning the yard and he asked me to help, I went along with him and helped. I wasn't expecting a reward, but I ended up getting ten dollars. I even felt good about myself.

My father is the person that I learned this belief from, because he is always helping people when they're in need. He does this with the intention of not getting something in return. One example is that he helps people with addiction. I have noticed that whenever he needs help, people gather around to help him. This has also showed me that what goes around comes around. I want my life to be like this. I too am always trying to help people in need. I think the reason why some people don't help is because they are afraid to get involved. They're probably scared that they are going to have to do extra work. I agree with John F. Kennedy when he said, "Ask not what your country can do for you, ask what you can do for your country." I think there would be fewer problems if, when we saw someone struggling, we helped them instead of just walking away and saying it's not our problem.

Elvis Rivera is fourteen years old. He is from San Francisco. He likes to draw cartoons, play soccer, go dirt biking, and play video games. He likes writing, but sometimes it's hard because he has to write in English at school and Spanish at home.

JALAPEÑOS AND BEST FRIENDS

BY ELVIS RIVERA

Do you remember when you had a best friend? Think about that day when you met your best friend. I'm going to tell a story about my best friend Jose, how we met and played. I think that friendship is the most important thing to me because, without friends, I wouldn't have as much fun. I believe in friendship and I think friendship should be about sharing stuff, having fun, and protecting each other as best friends.

I remember when Jose and I became best friends. In seventh grade, Jose and I became friends when I brought a burrito to school. Jose came up to me and said that he would give me five dollars if I gave him half of my burrito, but then I told him that I didn't want his money and gave him half of my burrito. Then he put jalapeños on it. After the first bite he was sniffing. I asked him if he needed water, but he said that he was okay. The second time I asked him if he needed to go to the bathroom, but he said he was okay again. The third time he ran to the bathroom to get water because it was really spicy. He was crying like a little baby. I was laughing so hard that I thought I was going to cry. I believe that when you share stuff you become best friends.

In seventh grade we spent every day together and played together. Sometimes we used to go to the store to get pizza or hot dogs. Then sometimes he told me that he wanted to stay at home, so sometimes on Fridays he didn't come to school. After school he came over to my house and we played together. His favorite game was Grand Theft Auto 5 and Black Ops 2 Zombies. Then at school we played soccer. I believe that you can always have fun with your friend.

Jose was like my security. Sometimes when he got really mad he used to punch the wall and he would start to bleed. Blood would come out of his hand because there were these kids named Gustavo, Rellovon, and Marvin who always wanted to fight with him because he was the tallest in the class. I helped Jose to feel better so he didn't fight with other people, and then I told him that the teacher was going to see and we were going to get in trouble. I think that this means that fighting doesn't help; only real friends can help you to do anything. If you're in trouble and you need help, they will be there for you.

This is why I'm so thankful to have Jose. But imagine if I didn't have someone who would be there for me. One time, I went to the park and I saw that there was a kid playing basketball. Then there was this other kid who came and took the ball away from him and started to play basketball without him. I thought that if Jose and I had been there, they wouldn't take the ball away from us because Jose is big and strong.

I think that people should believe in this so then some people could have good friendships. They could have more fun and they could have more friends. I think that some schools should be like this and should believe in this friendship. I feel bad that, when I graduated eighth grade, I went to Mission High School and my friends went to different schools, like Galileo High School, Washington High School, and Balboa High School. I think that schools should believe in friendship so that kids could be with the same friends that they had in their old school.

ELVIS RIVERA

I think that this is how you can make friends and have their backs. Sometimes, some people share some stuff and become best friends. They could have more fun and then other people would be more respectful and friendly. Friends are not only a way to have fun, because friends can also help you to get out of trouble. I think that this is how you can become friends and have each other's back.

Marcos Ochoa is a native San Franciscan, born and raised. The second of seven children, he's always down to try new things with his friends and family. A self-described "outside kind of guy," you'll probably find Marcos playing center on the Mission High School football team. Marcos lives by the sayings "Never give up on your dreams" and "Give respect to be respected." He also wants to let the world know that he once dated three girls at the same time.

MUSIC DREAMS

BY MARCOS OCHOA

Music has helped me through the years. When I was growing up, music helped me when my parents would argue and I would cry. The fighting started when I was little, about six years old. I remember when I would be in my room crying and telling myself, *When will the pain go away?* I felt like I wanted to stay in my room for years and never come out. It was a cold time in my life, but every time I felt lonely there was something that helped me. I used to listen to peaceful music, and it helped me not to cry. Music helped me be stronger and have the courage to keep my head up. But in the sixth grade, when I was eleven, I started noticing that I had a great passion for making music.

I didn't have friends to help me feel better emotionally, but by then I had an instrument. My instrument was a four-string instrument that made a groovy sound every time I played it. I dedicated my time to playing and enjoying the beauty of the sound as it relaxed my ears. It was very heavy when I held it and it wasn't a perfect fit at first. My instrument was a bass guitar. I learned how to play by myself, and I would use YouTube and the Internet to teach myself. I didn't care how long it took to learn. As long as I had the bass, I would love it. I would practice every day and sometimes at night. I still remember my mom telling me to go to sleep at 2 a.m. I love the bass so much that I still have it today. The bass used to be very heavy, but now I cannot feel its weight. I feel that I could carry the bass forever. My fingers know what to do every time I play it.

It was a Saturday in 2012; I was very excited because there was no school. Around 1 p.m., I was in my room making a new song. It was cold as a freezer, but I had called my friend to come to my house. My legs were cold and I ran out of marshmallows for my hot chocolate, but I didn't care because my friend was coming over. When my friend arrived he came running upstairs; his feet made a sound like a xylophone. When I saw him, he told me about a new album. It was called *Next Generation,* by a famous band called Aventura. The lead singer of the band, Aventura, was a young teenager that loved to talk about love. His style of music was *bachata,* a style that makes you want to dance and involves a lot of guitar. Bachata is a relaxing style of music that involves the bass. It also makes you want to dance. So many people inspired Aventura's music. He made a ton of songs, but one of my favorites was called "Llevame Contigo (Take Me with You)." This song talks about a boy begging his girlfriend to stay with him. Those songs were a big hit all over Central America and other places before they came here, and that's where I found the band Aventura. They inspired me.

I want to be a famous singer because I've been inspired throughout the years to write music. A song that I composed is called "Cuando Entenderas (When Will You Understand?)" "Cuando Entenderas" is about the love between a boy and a girl. The boy loves the girl, and he's telling her that he loves her and he wants her to be his girlfriend.

When I wrote music, I did it with my band. There were four people in my band. One of my friends introduced me to a couple other guys, and then we decided to start a band. One guy played the keyboard, another played the guitar. I played the bass and did the vocals, and Omar did backup vocals. Our band was called the Next

Ones. We played bachata. I used to live in the Mission, where there are a lot of Latino people, and a lot of people like bachata. We played bachata better than any other style. My band meant a lot to me because they were the missing part that I was looking for. Every time I played with them, it made me feel like they understood me, and I was happy that I had them with me. Every time we played made me feel very happy, and I wanted to play nonstop. The whole experience of being with my band was precious, and it made me want to stay forever.

I believe that I was born for music, and that music helps you feel better. It helps me when I struggle. I concentrate more on my work when I'm listening to music. It makes me happy and it's helped me throughout the years. I believe it can also help you.

Graeme Williams is fourteen years old and has called San Francisco home ever since he was a wee one. He loves his three older sisters slightly more than he loves the game of baseball. He's part Spanish, has some killer dance moves, and is an overall force to be reckoned with.

ALWAYS BRING YOUR UNIFORM

BY GRAEME WILLIAMS

It was Friday, my favorite day of the week, until I remembered: *I have Kennedy's class*. I checked my bag and I didn't see my PE uniform. I hoped one of my friends had a uniform I could borrow, but sadly no one did. I looked through my whole bag hoping to find it when I remembered I had left it on my bed. It was my first day of class and I was going to be late, without a uniform.

When I walked into the gym, everyone was looking at me and I felt embarrassed. Everyone had their nasty yellow uniforms that reminded me of rotten lemons, while I walked into the gym with jeans on. I accepted my fate, and I was waiting for the punishment. I was wondering what would happen. Because Kennedy was a former marine, I didn't know what was in store. Finally, he walked up to the podium that was almost as tall as he was. I could feel my stomach bubbling with heat; I was thinking of all the marine training he might make me do. As he called roll, kid by kid, getting closer to the W's, I could feel my heart beating over and over like an old school bell. I felt my hands sweating, and my head was pounding like a drum. Finally, he called my name.

"Graeme Williams."

"Here," I said.

He looked me up and down.

"Did we change our school uniform? Twenty-five."

Twenty-five push-ups. I didn't see that coming. I got on all fours and started doing push-ups. I could feel everyone staring at me. I finished my push-ups relieved, then I looked up at him and he told me, "Twenty-five."

"Again?" I asked, looking concerned.

"You were late too," he responded.

Once again, I got on all fours and started doing another set. I was going steady until I hit fifteen push-ups. Then I started slowing down, and shaking; my arms felt like they were going to fall off. Each time I pushed up, my arms burned more and more as if someone kept pouring lava on them. Immediately once I hit fifty push-ups I put my knees down and rested. Next time it'd be easier to bring my uniform.

Kennedy's class is tough, but it's even harder when you come unprepared. Bringing your uniform and wearing it makes his class so much easier. Being prepared doesn't only mean clothing for a PE class; preparation can be a pencil for school, studying for a quiz, or getting enough sleep for a big day. With any responsibility, coming prepared always makes it easier. Doing extra push-ups is not worth it if all you have to do to avoid it is bring a uniform.

For example, at my job, which is keeping score of kids' soccer games, coming early, getting the names of all the players, and keeping track of goals makes me happy and my boss happy. However, sometimes I come late and I miss key parts of the game, like goals and fouls. When this happens, I have to make up the scores of what I missed while trying to keep up with the current game. This doesn't usually turn out well because I make mistakes and then parents get mad at

"As he called roll, kid by kid, getting closer to the W's, I could feel my heart beating over and over like an old school bell. I felt my hands sweating, and my head was pounding like a drum. Finally, he called my name."

me. Believe me, soccer moms can be dangerous. In other words, it's impossible to do your job well if you come unprepared. If I came unprepared and late every time I had to go to my job, I wouldn't only be letting myself down, I'd be letting my coworkers and my boss down. I can choose how easy my job is going to be, and that means that I get enough sleep, come on time, eat breakfast, and get myself mentally prepared for the day.

If I didn't believe in coming prepared every day, or handling any responsibilities I have, then I'd never be successful. I have a friend who doesn't share this belief at all. I'm not sure what he cares about, because he doesn't come prepared to anything. He doesn't have any ambition for school, he never comes prepared for any responsibility, and all he wants to do is smoke weed. He doesn't understand that taking it easy and being carefree in school will ruin his future. Sure, he thinks it's fun right now to have no responsibility and to just go home and get high, but there's no job that requires you to smoke weed all day and not worry about anything.

In all truth, I don't come prepared to school every day or to my job every time. I'm not the most prepared person in the world by far. That doesn't mean I don't believe in coming prepared, and that coming prepared is really important, but sometimes there's a little too much going on in your life to remember all your responsibilities. For example, there've been a couple times I haven't done an essay, or I haven't always done my homework every day, and at my job I haven't always come on time. It's impossible to come prepared to every situation, because no one's perfect, and unless you can go back in time and fix every mistake you've ever made, you can't come prepared to everything. The most important thing you can prepare for is to be able to adapt.

Ever since my first day of Kennedy's class I learned how important it is to come prepared. Doing those push-ups, being watched by the whole class, feeling embarrassed, and getting harassed by soccer moms impacted my perspective on how to deal with my responsibilities. This belief applies to many people, and some don't even realize it. Without preparation, people would be lazy and unorganized. Bringing my uniform to PE class has taught me about ownership, and how it applies to everyday life. Whatever you do, make sure to bring your uniform, or else Kennedy's going to have you do push-ups.

Christopher Archilla's parents come from Guatemala, but he was born in San Francisco. Christopher is very afraid of dogs, because when he was three years old he was knocked over by a big brown dog while his family was in Guatemala. He was badly hurt and has been afraid of all dogs ever since. Christopher went to A.P. Giannini Middle School. He likes to sing at home with his friends. Chris has an amazing iPad and likes to play games on it. His favorite is FIFA 2014.

I BELIEVE IN LOVE

BY CHRISTOPHER ARCHILLA

I believe in love for many reasons. Once you love someone, you can never forget about it. Love gives you strength, even when someone is far away or dies. My girlfriend Delia lives far away in Guatemala, and I still love her. My father's brother, Uncle Chito, died in a motorcycle accident, but my whole family still loves him. My dad believes in love. When he met my mom in Guatemala, he knew he loved her. He has two kids that he loves, cares for, and supports by being there for all of us. I also believe in love because my pastor once told me, "Everyone at church loves you." This made me feel very happy. It makes me feel happy to be loved and to love others. I also developed love for music by learning to play the drums.

I believe in romantic love. When I started dating Delia, I was happy. I know that I will always have her by my side. She is happy when I sing a song about love, such as "Little Things" by One Direction. She starts to cry. It changed my life when I first met Delia when she was visiting my house. Later she helped me make my podcast. She started singing in my musical group, called the Christopher and Gerard Show. This is why I love her more and more. Our show starts with a special song. The song is called "One Thing," by One Direction. I gave Delia a special part to say about me. I hope that someday Delia will come here and that we will stay in love.

I love my family. I love my dad because he protects me, cares about me, and supports me. We go to my brother's house in Los Banos. I love my mom because she cooks for me, cares about me, and also talks with me and buys things for me. I love my sister. Her name is Jocelyn and she is twenty-one years old. She play-fights with me and also watches me when I play FIFA 2014 on the iPad. I love my brother Jonathan, who is twenty-eight years old, because he always says "I love you" to me. He fell in love with my sister-in-law, Anna, and they had a baby. I love my cousins, David and Diana, because they are always welcome at my house. I love my baby nephew, Jonathan, who is seven months old. He's cute, just like me—Christopher "Good-Looking Famous" Archilla. I love my whole family.

I believe in the love of music. I just started playing music with my two cousins, Diana and David. David is going to play the piano, I will play the drums, and Diana will sing. I've believed in my love of playing music ever since I was seven or eight years old. I wanted to play the drums, and so I will learn how to play drums and become a great drummer by practicing every day. In the eighth grade, my teacher told the assistant principal to call me Christopher "Famous," and I added "Good-Looking." This is my stage name.

One day, when I was thirteen, my uncle, his wife, and their two kids went to church. The pastor told me to come to the front and told me to get on the stage. There were drums there.

He taught me how to keep the rhythm and how to hit the drums. His name is Siverio and I learned to play by watching him. I would like to play onstage with him because we have two sets of drums. Someday, when I get really good, I would like to play at church on Sundays. Later, my mom bought me a karaoke machine so I could follow the song with my tabletop electronic drum set.

These experiences showed me that I believe in the love of music and always will.

I think that love is important because it makes me feel happy and also helps me. I love 826 Valencia because they helped Mr. Anders help us to write these essays. I loved writing this essay. I am happy about all the love in my life, which includes my love for Delia, my love for my family, and my special love for music. Love makes the world go around.

Elise Wise was born and raised in San Francisco, and loves dense, walkable cities where she can discover something new at every turn. At Mission High School, she's a member of the wrestling team and enjoys all her classes, especially history. Elise listens to music and hangs out with her friends whenever she has a chance.

A SMILE IS A GIFT

BY ELISE WISE

Most people in this world are happy—happy to be alive, happy to be with family and friends. Happiness is everywhere and anywhere. Most people are happy when they receive gifts and get all sorts of things, but I believe there is true happiness in giving, not receiving. You may be curious about why. I didn't always think this. I used to give and take without any meaning to it.

Before I figured out that happiness is in giving and not receiving, I always thought that if you gave something to someone or someone gave something to you, you would always have to return the favor. For example, when I was in elementary school, people would "kindly" give you their snacks or lunch and the next day you would have to pay them back with one of your snacks or a favor. I didn't know what giving was really about. I was constantly reminded by the environment of needing to return the favor, but that isn't always the case. Sometimes a simple thank-you will be enough to return the favor.

A couple months ago I was babysitting a family friend I always babysit, Abby. She is about seven years old, with long dark-brown hair and big brown eyes. She was over at my house on a Tuesday night. I was helping her with her math homework. My mom had made cookies that smelled like soft sugar and a warm fireplace. Abby kept taking the cookies and not saying one thank-you. I didn't think anything of it. The next morning I made her breakfast, helped her get dressed for school, made her lunch, and did not hear one thank-you. I felt a little disappointed. When I was her age I always said thank you, and it made my mom and others happy. Maybe she was never taught to help others and say thank you. It's weird how some kids and adults go about their day without finding happiness in a thank-you or a helping hand. So I had to tell her, "Sometimes a simple thank-you or a helpful gesture is enough to return the favor."

After I taught Abby that there is happiness in giving and in showing appreciation, she showed it more often. She is probably not the only person out there who doesn't know happiness is in giving. Kids nowadays have iPads, iPods, iPhones, all these gadgets. They don't really get to see the world as much as they should. Kids go to a park not to play on the playground, but to play on their iPad.

When I was Abby's age, like I said before, I was very naïve and I thought that I had to always give back. It was hard to really understand the concept of giving without expecting something in return. My mom was a big part of this. My mom always wanted me to learn that greed can lead to worse things, like self-obsession. Our faith in God really helped us through this. In the Bible, Jesus gave his blood and part of his body to his apostles. His whole life was based on kindness and giving. He always knew his happiness was in giving and even gave up his life for others. My mom also really wanted me to learn about this at a younger age so that I wouldn't have to question it later in my life, even though that didn't really happen. Sometimes learning the hard way can easily help us learn.

When I was little, my mom would always be kind to random strangers and smile at them. As a kid I thought that was weird and embarrassing, like peeing in your pants on the first day of kindergarten. She didn't know these people at all and yet she would spend her time being nice to them. I never truly understood why she did this until I came across the same situation.

I was in eighth grade and it was the summer before I was going to high school. My best friend Leila and I were heading toward downtown to do a little shopping. We met at my house and walked to the N Judah stop. We got on the train and didn't get off until Montgomery station. We got off and went to this new boba place in the Financial District before heading downtown. We ran back to Montgomery station like a stampede of wild elephants so we wouldn't miss our train, and we luckily made it. After we got on the train a homeless man in a wheelchair got on. I looked at him and smiled. He didn't seem to have anything on him but his old, ripped clothes. He wheeled across to where we were sitting and I couldn't help but reach out my wallet and give him the rest of my money. I said, "This is all I have left." He smiled at me since nobody else, not even Leila, gave him anything. He looked at me and said, "God bless you, child." Leila looked at me like I had done something crazy.

"Why'd you give him the rest of your money?" Leila said.

"Because it made him happy and me happier," I said.

She smiled at me and said, "That's why we're friends."

I laughed and responded, "Yeah, you're probably really lucky to have me."

This moment really triggered something good inside me. I didn't know what it was about this moment that made me feel so good about myself, but it made me realize that moments like these can really change a person and how they feel about life. I'm still growing as a person and discovering new things as I go. I hope to have more moments like this one, where I can feel happy to know I made someone else happy by doing something so simple.

Ricardo Escalante was born in El Salvador and moved to San Francisco with his two brothers when he was seven. He is now fifteen. He loves funky music and plays bass guitar in a band. He also loves soccer and eating everything... except vegetables.

THE BIG CHANGE

BY RICARDO ESCALANTE

I was walking to the counselor's office. I was in the hallway, only looking down because I knew what I had done and was thinking about the consequences. The counselor's room was hot and small. I saw that my mom was mad and the counselor was really serious. My mom gave the angry eyes and I knew I was in a lot of trouble. The counselor told me to sit down. Then she asked me, "Do you know why you are here?" to which I said, "Yes." She said to tell her why I was there. I told her it was because I had gotten into a fight. My mom said that she wasn't feeling that good and I was making it worse with my behavior. She worked so she could buy me things I needed for school. She felt like she had been working hard to buy me things I was not using, like it was all for nothing. She started to cry and I didn't want to look at her because it made me feel bad. I was just looking around the counselor's room, hoping that they could open the window so I could relax more and my mom could get some air. The counselor asked me if I was okay, because I looked lost. I said yes but I truly felt bad. When I got home, my mom just went to bed. This made me feel disappointed, deeply sad, and guilty for what I had done. I felt like this because she had just got surgery a few weeks before.

I got in trouble often in middle school. I liked to skip classes with some kids named Giovanni, Skinny Pedro, Fat Pedro, Peter, Kelvin, Rigo, and Isabella (she's Skinny Pedro's girlfriend). I would leave class even if they were teaching. I didn't listen to the teachers. Students always wanted to fight me during lunch. They were always saying that they were going to beat me up, and I just made them more mad. They would throw the first punch, and after they'd throw that first punch, I wouldn't think about it; I would just throw the second punch, and I would hit like a hammer. The other students, including my friends, would watch me, but when they saw that the other kid couldn't fight anymore, they would tell me to stop and grab me. My brother was like me. He used to get into fights and sometimes he would get jumped. He would sometimes come home bleeding from his mouth or nose.

I was thinking about all this, and I was thinking about whether I should change or stay the same. My mom was the reason I wanted to change. Seeing her cry and just seeing her feel bad only made me sad, and I wished to be different. So I decided to change completely and be better. That's when I started to believe that "Darkness cannot drive out darkness, only light can. Hate cannot drive out hate, only love can." I thought to myself, *Bad cannot drive out bad, only the good can.*

I started to change, but it was hard. It wasn't fun; it was really boring and really tiring, and sometimes I felt sleepy. I kept trying to pay attention in my classes every day. I changed my friends and started to hang out with soccer players. I also stopped fighting. When others were bothering me and wanted to fight, I would just walk away. I was trying to be like a student that gets good grades and gets a diploma for their hard work, in order to make my family proud of me. I wanted to be a light in school and everywhere I went. Weeks and months passed and it was getting easier for me. I was becoming a different person—a good person, I guess.

One part that I changed is that I didn't let my friends fight— I stopped them. For example, my friend Pedro had an enemy named Giovanni and always wanted to fight. Giovanni was a bully; he messed with everybody. One day, Giovanni started to bother Pedro and Pedro got really mad. Pedro pushed Giovanni and they were getting ready to fight. Pedro's girlfriend ran up to me. She looked scared and worried, with her eyes wide open. She started to talk really fast. I didn't understand what they were saying, so I said to say it slower and relax. She said, "Okay," then spoke slower. She said that Pedro was about to fight. I asked her where Pedro was, and she said, "On the bridge."

I ran like a cheetah until I got to the bridge where I saw all the students, like a pack of wolves, waiting for them to fight. I started to push the people that were making the circle. I kept bumping into them and finally made it to the front. I grabbed Pedro and another friend grabbed Giovanni. I looked up so I could take Pedro out of the bridge and to a different area. Instead I saw every student screaming, "Fight, Fight, Fight," like it was a protest. I wanted to take Pedro away, but the bridge was too small, so I tried to convince Pedro not to listen to the crowd. He ignored me. I told him that he would get in trouble and his girlfriend was going to get mad, but he didn't care. He made up his mind and kept pushing me so he could throw the first punch. Students were saying to let go of him so he could fight, and I kept saying "No!" I started to push Pedro to get him out and other friends of his tried to help. They couldn't move Pedro because Pedro was big and they were small and weak. Pedro was like a wall for them. I had to do it. When I got him out, my other friend took Giovanni in the opposite direction. I stayed with Pedro on the bench until he calmed down. I think people can change. I think it's possible that they can become light in the way that they can do things that are not bad.

I think people should believe in my belief because the world would be better. There would be less fighting and less trouble—everything

"This would make the world better, just like Dr. Martin Luther King Jr. wanted. He was the one who said that 'Darkness cannot drive out darkness, only light can. Hate cannot drive out hate, only love can.'"

would be better. I stand by this belief because it helped me a lot in my life and it changed me. I think it can change you too. You would be able to forgive people easier, solve problems, respect more, and help other people. This would make the world better, just like Dr. Martin Luther King Jr. wanted. He was the one who said that "Darkness cannot drive out darkness, only light can. Hate cannot drive out hate, only love can." I think Dr. Martin Luther King Jr. was trying to say to stop the violence, racism, and the wars.

My parents and my older brother believe in this belief because there are some people who treat them horribly. Later, when the people that treated my family poorly ask for help, my family will help them because they forgive them. I know a friend who doesn't believe in this and he is always in a bad mood or holding a grudge, and people don't like him.

I think the world would be so much better and everyone would be like my family if they embraced my belief. But if you don't, I think it would look like the end of the world. So, do you want to believe or not?

Mateo Zelaya is a fifteen-year-old from San Francisco. He enjoys the original Star Wars trilogy and Marvel movies. His favorite superhero is Batman because he fights for justice and has awesome gadgets. He cares a lot about his family and friends.

LEARNING AT SCHOOL

BY MATEO ZELAYA

I believe that school is a good place to learn. I started believing this when I first started going to school. I go to Mission High School. My school is a big white building with a tall tower. Inside the building there are computer labs, students, hallways, teachers, classrooms, and a huge auditorium. And the bell isn't too loud at Mission. The bell sounds like a soft electronic beep. I like my school because it's easy to walk to, my dad works here, and I know how to take the bus to my dad's house. My classes range from easy to fine. Some of my classes are English, geography, life skills, and PE. My teachers are nice to me because they help me and show me that I am doing a great job.

Every morning I eat breakfast and then I walk to school. It doesn't take very long. My day starts with different classes. I see a lot of people at school walking and talking. When I get to class, I sit at my desk and take out my pencil. Sometimes I get prepared for class. Then I listen to the teacher and learn new things. At lunch I go to the cafeteria and eat my lunch. Sometimes I bring my peanut-butter-and-jelly sandwich to school when I have lunch. After lunch, I go to the library and look at some comic books, like Batman or Marvel. I enjoy reading. And when lunchtime is over, I go to math or media arts. At the end of the school day, I go home. I often learn a lot of stuff.

"I believe that school is a good place to learn. I have been going to school for ten years, and I have learned a lot. I am in high school now. I want to go to college because it's about learning and getting smarter. I think everyone should share my belief about schools."

I have learned about Martin Luther King Jr. in my class. I watched his speech, and he was a good man. He was very brave, and he helped his people. I learned that his family was brave too. He wanted African Americans to be free. In the 1960s, African Americans were treated badly. I like learning about history. Learning about people from history is important because you can learn stories about good people from the past. Abraham Lincoln is another example, because he ended slavery and he was a good president. We should try to be excellent people like them.

I also learned about math in school. I know about greater-than and less-than. And I also know about adding and taking away. Math is sometimes hard; it's kind of confusing when you learn new things. I feel lost when I don't get it. Even when it's hard, I still try because I want to get better at it.

I believe that school is a good place to learn. I have been going to school for ten years, and I have learned a lot. I am in high school now. I want to go to college because it's about learning and getting smarter. My parents work in high schools. I think everyone should share my belief about schools. If they did, the world would be a better place because people would be happy and smarter.

Sam Flores is proud to have graduated from St. Leander school and to have started his freshman year at Mission High in September 2014. Sam was born in San Lorenzo, California, and moved to San Francisco with his mom and stepdad in July 2014. He loves to go out to eat, especially burritos, followed by a nice long nap. He never leaves the house without his phone so he can listen to his favorite R&B Queen B, Beyoncé. If he could have a superpower, he would teleport himself in time and space to L.A. in the 90s, and he would dress like the Fresh Prince of Bel Air.

FRIENDS ARE THE BEST INVESTMENT

BY SAM FLORES

I believe when we make friends and family a priority, we remember what's really important in life.

Even though at times things in life can be challenging, you can look on the bright side. For example, learning about current events could be depressing, but friends can always make it better. One day in Ethnic Studies, Ms. Reyes was standing in front of the room, telling us about what had happened in Ferguson. I felt helpless because a lot of people were injured in riots while they were trying to make a difference. I also felt frustrated knowing that someone had died just because of his race. Later, when I was talking with my old friends from middle school, we were all texting each other about what was happening in Ferguson. I felt so relieved because it was such a serious topic to talk about. I also felt grateful to have friends so I could share my feelings about it. Even in serious situations, friends can make everything better or okay.

I believe that friendship can make anything fun. When you have friends, you can just do anything, whether it's telling stories, listening to music, going on the Internet, looking through old pictures, or telling jokes. There are a whole lot of ideas to come up with when it comes to being friends, while having fun at the same time. When I hang out with friends in school, I feel that I can share whatever is on my mind, and that makes me happy. For example, when I listen to music and sing along with a friend, I also feel free. When my friends and I check out cool music videos, sometimes I feel excited or curious to see something new. Sometimes, when I look through old pictures with my friends, I feel closer to them. It's special because not everyone gets to see those pictures. It also makes me realize how important it is to share things that are personal with people I care about, or people I trust. I can really be myself around my friends, and that makes me feel like having fun is possible.

Even in the times when it could be easy to take friends and family for granted, you can be reminded how important they are. One weekend, when I was at Pier 39 with my family, I got to share some really cool stuff with my cousins. To make it fun, we took some pictures on the new digital camera I got from Amazon. It was a pretty cool camera, kind of like a Polaroid. You take the picture and it instantly comes out of the top of the camera. We took a picture of us in front of Alcatraz and, when the picture came out, I let it develop before I showed it to them. It was fun to see that they were impressed by an old-fashioned way of taking pictures. Afterward, when I got home, I put the pictures on my wall so I could remember all the moments in that day I had with my family and the places we visited. I'm reminded, when I see my cousins in those photos on my wall, that I always have someone to keep me company and share fun stuff with.

Whether you find yourself dealing with a serious situation, or even if it's just a regular day, when you focus on friendship and share your feelings, you remember that freedom, possibility, happiness, and fun are just a moment away. When you're there for your friends, no matter what the situation is, friends will always be there for you.

SAM FLORES

"I felt so relieved because it was such a serious topic to talk about."

Malik Miller was born in Modesto, California, but has spent most of his life in San Francisco. He loves his friends and family, and after high school he wants to study engineering at UCLA so he can help his family and others. When he is not in school, he enjoys spending time with his friends and playing football. If he could go anywhere in the world, he would go to the Bahamas because he has heard it is beautiful.

BREAK BREAD

BY MALIK MILLER

"If you don't break bread, you fake." This means that if you don't share what you have, then you are not real. This belief has made me and my friends closer and closer. I say that because me and my friends shared almost everything. My friends and I became like brothers. We shared everything and anything: lunch, money, and we sometimes even like the same girls; we don't care. Nothing is mine; it's ours.

I've known my friends since we were very young, and we started sharing stuff around fifth grade. It started when I was so hungry and my friend's mom bought him a Subway sandwich. He knew I was hungry, so he gave me half of his Subway sandwich. If he didn't give me that half, I would have died from starvation or something. After that moment, I felt like I owed him back. Since that point, we have also shared fun together; we always try to be together.

It was a warm summer day, June 17, two days before my birthday. I was so excited, but I didn't know what I was doing because my mom said it was a surprise. I got a call from my new phone that my mom had already bought as an early gift. I answered it and she said, "Pack your things."

I asked, "For what? Where are we going?"

She answered back, "You and I are going to Magic Mountain."

I was so excited that I hurried to my closet and just started putting stuff in my green duffel bag. As soon as she got home, I asked if I could bring one of my friends, Joseph. She looked at me strangely. She thought I was playing, but then she realized that I was serious, so she said okay. I was so juiced. I hurried up the stairs and called my friend to tell him the good news, and to see if his parents would let him go. His parents said okay, and the next day his mom dropped him off at my house. He slept over so we could wake up early in the morning.

The next morning, we hit the road. We picked up my mom's friend so he could drive us, because my mom drives like a sloth, and her friend drives faster. The drive was the best part, to be honest, all because of my mom's friend. I call him Big James. We played road-trip games over and over. For example, we played I Spy, an alphabet game where we had to name off an animal for each letter, and "who can read the signs the fastest." But my favorite game was I Spy because I never lost. We stopped at truck stops and we ate so much food from Wendy's that my belly was about to pop. When we got to Los Angeles, we dropped off Big James at his hotel and we said our good-byes. Then we drove to our hotel. That was the worst part, because we had to wait so long because our room wasn't ready.

Afterward we went to the amusement park, Magic Mountain. We got on every single ride we could see. Joseph was scared of roller coasters, but I helped him conquer his fear. Our favorite roller coaster was called the Viper. It was red and white and it went really fast. When we went on the dip, it went so fast I could feel tears coming down my face.

It was Joseph's first time in Los Angeles and at Magic Mountain, so we showed him everything in L.A. that we know. I was glad to show my best friend everything, to hear everything and taste everything. We showed him Hollywood Boulevard, and we took a lot of pictures of us near the celebrity stars. After that, we went to Venice Beach and saw a man who was playing Tupac on this enormous black speaker so that everyone could hear. We sat near the music and listened to it, because Tupac is my mom's favorite artist.

Finally, we went to Roscoe's Chicken 'n Waffles; I was pumped up for that one because I had saved my appetite just for that. It was a long wait because there were a lot of people in line, but as soon as my mom's name was called, I rushed to the door. When I first walked in, all I could smell was grease. I could hear people saying "Order up!" and see families eating like pigs. My friend didn't know what to order, so I showed him the Obama's Plate, which had three pieces of chicken and three waffles with any side. That's what I always get when I go to Roscoe's. I choose that dish all the time because their waffles are the best; it's like God made them. That was my best birthday ever, and I was happy to share it with one of my best friends. Inviting my friend to share this experience is an example of how breaking bread made us even closer. Without that belief, we wouldn't experience as many things together.

Before, when I didn't believe in this belief, I was a selfish brat and I didn't share anything. I was like that because when my mom packed me lunch, she always told me, "This lunch is only for you." During weekends I used to go outside with my bike and my mom told me, "Don't let nobody ride your bike or they will steal it." I was like that with every belonging I had. I was just plain stingy. I didn't share any of my footballs, even though I had like four of them. My mom taught me to not share because people in the world steal a lot of things. That's what my mom always told me. One time, there was a family get-together and I was about four or five, so I was pretty young. My cousins and my uncles wanted to play football, but they didn't have a ball. Inside of my mom's green Honda I always kept a football by my gray car seat. They asked me if they could use it. I said, "No, it's mine." But then my mom yelled at me, so I was forced to give it to them. It was different when I was young because when I was young, I didn't trust anybody the way I trust my friends now. Trusting made my life better because my friends and I got closer and closer.

My mom really didn't know my belief. One time in eighth grade, she gave me ten dollars on a Friday. After school I bought myself and my friends some cookies, and I wasted all of my money in one day. I got home and my mom asked me how much I had left. I answered, "Nothing." She started yelling at me. She yelled, "What did you buy to waste all of your money in one day?!" I said, "My friends and I went to the store and I was the only one with money, so I bought all of us some cookies." She asked me why, and I explained to her my belief. I said that my friends are like my second family, and my mom always told me to share everything with your family. If you have close friends like I do you will always get paid back because we are not selfish. My mom understood and I could tell that she learned from it. My belief is that everything you have is to share. My mom's version of my belief is that if you have enough to share, then you can share.

Sometimes it can be difficult to break bread because we don't always have money. This school year, my mom and my stepdad weren't making enough money to give me some in my pocket every day. My dad wasn't around, and he mostly gives me money for my pocket. My mom also wasn't giving me money like she used to, so I was broke as a joke almost every day. Every day after school my friends would go to the store by my house. They knew my pockets were empty, so they just bought me a bag of chips and a fifty-cent soda almost every time I was there. When my other friend Justin

MALIK MILLER

gets Fanta, instead of getting a bottle, he gets a two-liter so he can share with all of us. Another time, when Joseph and I were hungry, he bought a big plate of Chinese food and we shared that. I respect and love my friends to death. They are like my brothers, and without them I don't know where I would be. The challenging part about my belief was when I didn't have enough money for my friends; it was only enough for me. I only had two dollars. I felt stuck. I didn't know what to do, to be honest, so we all got fifty-cent honey buns. We weren't really full; we were still hungry, but it was better than nothing.

My belief matters to me so much because that belief made me and my friends closer. Without that belief, we wouldn't be really close like that. I think this should matter to everyone, so you can see who in your life is fake and who's real. What I'm saying is that if you are a real friend, you will do however much you can to give some of what you've got to your best friends.

THE COMPASS WITHIN

STORIES OF CHANGE

Ana Sara Malaquias was born in Uberlandia, Brazil. She came to San Francisco when she was ten, not knowing one word of English. Ana Sara can be found late at night curled up with her Kindle, voraciously reading or watching a horror film on Netflix. She's known for her baking—particularly her cookies—and is devoted to her one-year-old sister Kiata. In addition to juggling her studies, family, and friends, she plays volleyball and soccer.

COMFORT ISN'T EVERYTHING

BY ANA SARA MALAQUIAS

What holds people back from trying something unfamiliar and pursuing their dreams?

When I was ten, my dad convinced me that I would have better opportunities if I came to the United States and lived with my mom. He said I would have better access to a good education, better job opportunities, and a better way of living too. But coming here meant getting way out of my comfort zone, leaving my family, friends, my country, and the only language I knew, and having to learn English. With the overwhelming desire to be successful, I went for it.

In 2010, I was a newcomer and jumped into fifth grade without finishing fourth grade in Brazil, and without knowing any English. During the first two weeks I attended school, my mom sat with me for half of the day and translated what the teacher was saying into Portuguese. At first just sitting there and not knowing what was going on was mind-numbing, but as I caught on it became more engaging. After my mom went back to work full-time, the two girls who sat at my table translated the teacher's instructions into Spanish, which I was able to understand well enough to start getting more familiar with English.

I remember getting pulled out of class every day to go with the English teacher, and she would take us to her big white room. It had a bunch of books, desks, and some materials such as colored pencils, glue sticks, paper, erasers, and a colorful mat that we would sit on when she told us stories. Also, she had signs for everything in the room so we could become more familiar with the objects. From pencils to the desks—you name it, she had it labeled. Every time I walked in there, I could smell the cold, clean air; I felt nervous and impatient because I didn't know a single word in English and couldn't wait until I finally learned it. I remember feeling the hardcover books that she would give us to read out loud. They were beginning-reader books that talked about the colors, emotions, and fruits. The teacher would sound out every syllable of every word so we could do the same.

I thought that I could also read to myself at home, so I asked my mom to go with me to the library to check out some books. Right away we found a book translated from Portuguese to English. I got that one and a few other books in English. I would read those books every night and even talk to my mom in English.

In addition, I started to go to the YMCA after-school program near my house and I would practice my English there too. It was helpful because we had one-on-one tutors to go over our homework with us. This gave me more confidence in school because I knew when I walked in to school every day my homework was complete and correct.

Fifth grade was almost over before I realized that I had learned how to read, write, and speak in English. I called my dad in Brazil to tell him how I was doing. I spoke with him in Portuguese and he asked me how to say a few things in English, and I taught him how to say them. He told me that he was proud of me. My dad's reaction made me understand what a huge accomplishment it was. That made me realize that if I set my mind to do something new I can achieve it. Here I was, a ten-year-old kid, speaking English, something my dad couldn't even do. I started to even dream in English, which is weird to think about!

That's when I understood that getting out of my comfort zone could change my view of myself. That's the first step to changing your path in life.

Last year in eighth grade I got out of my comfort zone again and tried out for a soccer team at my middle school. Brazilians know all about soccer, right? Wrong. At least not this Brazilian. I didn't know the first thing about soccer: how to pass the ball, the positions, the rules—I didn't even know about cleats! The coach was really friendly and easy to relate to because he was in his twenties. He was funny in a goofy kind of way, and could relate to us because he had a sister about our age. Most of the girls welcomed me, even though I didn't know much about soccer.

It was really tough for me to keep up, because most of the girls had played since kindergarten. They knew everything: how to pass the ball, how to make a goal, how to defend, and how to do some tricks as well. Seeing them really discouraged me at first. I kept telling myself that it was in my Brazilian DNA, and my coach was encouraging. He would say, "Don't quit, because you can get better with time." Every time I put myself down he'd say, "Don't worry about everyone else; they've been playing since they were little and you've just started." Even now I remember that when I'm trying to learn more advanced techniques in soccer.

I was really nervous the day of my first game. I went to the bathroom about a hundred times that day, I had butterflies in my stomach, and I was worried I'd be late for the game or not have all my equipment. When we got to the field, the first thing I noticed was the green turf grass; it almost seemed as if it was quicksand. There was no one on the sidelines besides the players and their coaches. My coach put me in as a starter in middle defense. My good friend was also in defense, and helped by telling me what to do for the whole game. Her constant patter of suggestions encouraged me. Whenever I did something right, she would compliment me, and if I made a mistake she would tell me to just shake it off. After the first twenty minutes, I was able to relax and realized, "Okay, I can do this—just keep the ball away from the goal!"

I'm still playing soccer and I'm still learning. I can juggle four bounces so far, and I'm determined to do more. Playing soccer has taught me to not give up, and to set my mind on my goals. It's certainly surprising that coming to the United States led to me learning all about soccer, and feeling more Brazilian. Living here has helped me realize how cool and different it is to be from Brazil, and I really embrace my culture now.

I think that what holds people back from getting out of their comfort zone is fear of what others might think or say. If you question your abilities, it's much easier for the negative opinion of others to affect you. If you really set your mind to it, you can overcome fear, insecurity, and the opinions of others.

Becoming fluent in English and then later trying out for the soccer team helped me see myself differently. I'm no longer that quiet girl who wasn't very good at school; now I'm a good student and I'm not afraid to try new things that interest me. I wish I could tell that ten-year-old girl who left Brazil this: "Don't be afraid of failing. Getting out of your comfort zone means that you're going to experience new and great things and learn a lot about yourself. You'll learn from your successes and your mistakes, and grow into the person you want to be."

ANA SARA MALAQUIAS

"Don't be afraid of failing."

Jamir Dreher, aka Numbers, was born in Berkeley, California. If he had a superpower it would be to stop time to catch up on sleep. If he were to sum up his feelings about writing with one word, it would be "different." If he had a thousand dollars he would travel from coast to coast.

TAKE A CHANCE

BY JAMIR DREHER

Before I believed in second chances, my life was heading down the wrong path. As my mother told me, "If you keep on this road, there are only two ways out: dead or in prison." At the time, I was in elementary school and didn't think about it. Now I know that if it weren't for second chances, my life would be wild and out of control. And I've seen a lot of people get out of control. I have seen fights, thefts, drive-by shooters, and I've lost a friend to murder.

I will never forget the night of my friend's death as long as I live. I was in bed asleep and something woke me up. I checked the time on my phone. It was 4 a.m., and I saw many text messages saying, "Shawn's dead." I was shocked and didn't know what to do or say. It was so unbelievable. At first, I started to cry, then I realized who could have killed Shawn. That was a real wake-up call for me. The first thought I had was retaliation. Then I figured it wouldn't bring him back.

Before I lost my friend, I used to be involved with a crowd that made dangerous choices. It started with bringing knives to school in third grade. By the time I got to middle school, the behavior got worse. I got suspended the second week of school, but still didn't stop. Instead I brought BB guns and stashed them in unused lockers all over school. This final act was the end of my crime-making career. This was when I got caught.

I should have known that you can't trust everyone. Someone snitched about the guns that we had, and the police showed up. They asked us to sit down and asked tons of questions about what we were doing, like who had the guns and why. Then I had to call my mother to come pick me up. If she hadn't come I would have been shoved into a dirty, cold, hard cell for the rest of the night.

When my mother came, I watched her talk to the police officer and knew the game was over. All the bad things I had done caught up with me. My mother was so frustrated to see her son surrounded by police. With her hands crossed as tight as a sailor's knot, I could tell she wasn't defending me. She called my father to pick me up.

It didn't take me long to realize it was time to change, but I didn't change right then. Some things that influenced me to change were a new school with new people who didn't have the same attitude as the old friends. I had to try something new. I already knew what the other path would do for me.

Since I've made the decision to change, my grades have improved and I stopped hanging with my old friends. And if I hadn't taken advantage of a new opportunity at a new school and had a fresh start, I might not have had taken this second chance. My mother's theory would have been right and I would have been stuck in a boiling pot of water with no way to cool down.

Some people don't have the opportunity or the will to change. Others are afraid to change or try new things because they're comfortable with their usual routines. For example, a student cheats on the state exam and he gets caught by the teacher. Yet he still cheats on the next test. If this student had taken the opportunity to change the first time he got caught cheating, he wouldn't have had to retake the test. Taking advantage of a second chance made me realize that I could change in a positive way and improve my life.

JAMIR DREHER

"My mother's theory would have been right and I would have been stuck in a boiling pot of water with no way to cool down."

Henry Bradley would like to be a superhero, so he could fly to Duc Loi super market on 18th Street and get some *banh mi*. Henry was born on December 23, 1999. He has an older brother and lives in Potrero Hill. In addition to having a sophisticated palate, he enjoys sports (he knows teams, stats, and players), learning about space, and baking. He's had a few fish in his lifetime, but unfortunately they all had to be flushed down the toilet. He once built a computer, and hopes to become an engineer one day.

GETTING OUT OF YOUR COMFORT ZONE: WHERE THE MAGIC HAPPENS

BY HENRY BRADLEY

After twelve hours of driving, we had finally arrived at the Grand Canyon. After all these months of dreading the trip, I was here, and there was no going back. But there was one thing I was curious about: I couldn't see the Canyon anywhere. All I saw was the arid terrain of Arizona, a few mountains off in the distance, and twisted bushes and trees that extended along the road and further out into the landscape. I remember how excited my mom was; she was like a hungry hipster walking into Chez Panisse for the first time. Unlike me, she couldn't wait for the backpacking trip into the depths of the Grand Canyon. She had been trying for weeks to force me to realize that it was going to be fun. I felt like there was no way that I could have fun, especially since the trip was during Thanksgiving, so I would miss all the deliciousness of home.

As we pulled into the more developed area around the Canyon, with parking lots, visitor centers, and paved roads, I was still surprised that no matter where I looked, I couldn't see the Canyon. When I got my stuff together, I started trying to follow my belief: getting out of your comfort zone gets you places. Surprisingly, it was quite cold outside, as cold as my hometown of San Francisco. I pulled my pack on, and I was happy to remember how light I had made it. Our goal for the day was simple: get halfway down.

Before my trip to the Grand Canyon, there had been a meeting about where everyone would camp. I missed that meeting. Since I wasn't there, they put me into the group that was going halfway down rather than all the way down to the river. I accepted that decision, since I knew that going to the halfway camp would be a lot easier and I would be more comfortable.

A few years prior to the trip, my mom had talked to me about my nervousness and inability to escape my comfort zone. I remember that I had just whined about something that I really didn't want to do, probably some after-school program involving a lot of time and physical exertion. Tilting her head in disappointment, she sat down at our dining room table and said, "You have to learn to do things you aren't comfortable with doing. You can't get by with only doing stuff you want to do. That won't get you anywhere in life." I knew what she meant, but I felt incapable of emerging from my comfort zone. Traditionally, I've been shy, and as far as physical exertion goes, I'm more of a sports fan than a player.

I remember when I was younger (seven or eight), I was invited to a birthday party. I didn't know the birthday girl very well, so I was nervous. My dad took me to her house in his truck. When we got there, I couldn't even make it halfway up the stairs. No matter how many promises he made about how fun it would be, I wouldn't go. I remember sitting in my dad's truck, almost physically unable to bring myself into the party. I was like a lonely spoon lying on the street, pathetically separated from its silverware-drawer compatriots. Even though I heard the delighted screams of friends that I was comfortable with, I refused to go. So eventually my dad gave in and took me home.

Obviously, this was an issue that I needed to work on.

After pulling on my pack, we started to head toward the start of the trail. Suddenly, after weaving our way past the buildings and trees, the Grand Canyon appeared before us. We took a minute to take in the sight. It was massive—bigger than any photo I had seen of it. The Canyon extended as far as the eye could see, in bands of bright reds, browns, and oranges. *Hey,* I thought, *this might not be so bad after all.*

We started down the trail, and we were a little overwhelmed by all the people. There was a big contrast between my group and the tourists: us with our massive backpacks and hiking boots, and them with their flip-flops and plastic water bottles. I could see the general area where we were headed, but it was a much longer hike down than I had expected. The trail zigzagged back and forth, making it longer than if it went straight down. However, it was still a pretty quick hike. We arrived at our campsite, Indian Garden, at about 2 p.m. It was covered in trees that were full of bright-yellow leaves. After setting up camp I was still energetic and there was a lot of time left in the day, so my dad and I went to explore the area. While we were exploring, we discussed a decision that I would have to make. Although I had been planning to stay in the middle for the second night of the trip, if I wanted to, I could camp at the bottom of the Canyon. When the decision was made for me to camp in the middle the first night, I had accepted that, since I knew it would be a lot easier hiking back up in two parts. But now I had another chance to go all the way. I still couldn't decide if I wanted to take the risk of sleeping at the bottom, since we would have to go all the way back up in a single day. I couldn't stop thinking about lagging behind the other hikers and slowing them down. If that were to happen I would be very embarrassed.

The next day, my group went down to the river to visit the others for a day hike, and we would return later on in the afternoon to go back to the middle campsite. Although I hadn't made the decision whether to camp at the bottom yet, I brought all my stuff so I would be prepared. I was the first to the river by a long shot, which showed me how much more advanced I was than the rest of my group, and how if I stayed with the bottom group I would have people who were on my level. At the river, the sand was unexpectedly soft. It was obvious that swimming in the river wouldn't be a good idea, because the water was so swift. But the sounds coming from the river were very relaxing and calming. My mom said that the river created great white noise for ease of sleep. "If you camp down here, you'll be able to say that you've camped at the bottom of the Grand Canyon. Not too many people can say that," my mom said.

That solidified my decision to stay at the bottom. I knew how tough the hike back up would be, but the rewards were too appealing to turn down. "Okay. I'll stay down here," I said.

I slept down at the bottom that night. My mom was right; the river did make really good white noise, with the rushing of the water echoing off the canyon walls. The next morning, we woke up before first light and crossed a bridge across the river. The water rushing under us was surreal, since we all knew that it was there but we couldn't see it since it was still black as pitch. I realized that if I had camped in the middle the second night, I would have missed that whole experience. The hike up was easier than I expected, since I knew how far up it was. Soon, we had passed the other group as they were struggling up the trail to the top.

Right when I stepped on the asphalt at the top of the Canyon, I was awash with the feelings of relief and accomplishment. The Dr. Pepper I had at the Canyon convenience store was one of the sweetest I'd ever had. I was not comfortable. I was sweaty, dirty, and my hair was matted. My feet felt like they would fall off if I took another step, my hips were raw and my shoulders were numb from the backpack, and my quads felt shredded. But somehow I felt comfortable with being uncomfortable.

I know that everyone who has a fulfilled life maintains that they're there because they took risks in their lives instead of playing it safe. For example, professional sports players became great by being comfortable with being uncomfortable. They took a risk by working harder even in difficult times. Furthermore, in almost every adventure story, the adventure is started by someone taking a risk instead of staying safe in their comfortable lives. Bilbo Baggins didn't want to leave the Shire because he was living in comfort. But rather than regretting not having taken the chance to go on an adventure, he decided to just go. And he had one of the greatest experiences of his life!

Like Bilbo, I took a risk by going on an adventure to the depths of the Grand Canyon. In the end, it changed me. Getting out of your comfort zone gets you places. The higher the risk, the higher the reward.

Alejandra Galvan is fourteen years old and was born and raised in the Mission District of San Francisco. She has an older brother, Jessie, as well as two adorable pet turtles, Betty and Scottie. If you want to get on her good side, offer her a Nutella sandwich. Alejandra is also very creative—she loves drawing, listening to all types of music, and the colors light green and lavender. Alejandra also has a knack for makeup; she hopes to have her own makeup line one day.

WHY A LITTLE TROUBLE ISN'T SUCH A BAD THING

BY ALEJANDRA GALVAN

In sixth grade we had a parent-teacher conference. "Since you're a nanny, you should just take her out of the school system and make her go to work with you," the teachers said to my mom. I couldn't believe it. I was only in sixth grade, but it seemed they'd already given up on me.

The parent-teacher conference had been planned to discuss my behavior in school. Two of my teachers, my mom, and the counselor were there. The teachers kept telling my mom how rude and disrespectful I was to them. When they spoke, their tone was excessively and unnecessarily aggressive. When I would try to explain myself, they would just interrupt and say bad things about me, telling me I wasn't going to do anything with my life if I kept being the way I was. I knew part of the reason for my behavior was because I didn't get attention from the teachers, and when I'd behave badly, that was the only time they would pay attention to me.

After that meeting, I felt really frustrated and mad because teachers aren't supposed to have that type of mentality toward students, even if they're not the best students. That meeting had been a low point for me, but later I would realize it was just one part of the path that would result in me figuring out what I believe and helping me to learn and grow.

When I was younger, I was hyper and social. With my big eyes and pale, clear skin, I was like a porcelain doll that was also energetic and really talkative to everyone. I would also sing to myself a lot.

But as the years went by, and as fifth grade was ending, I started doubting myself. The doubt and the pressure of school were hard on me, and they caused me to become a different, more defensive person. When middle school began I had my guard up and kept to myself like a brick wall. I wouldn't pay attention to other people, and if they tried talking to me I'd keep the conversation short. During sixth grade I would get referrals, phone calls home, detention. Anything that meant trouble, I was there.

Because of these negative interactions, it seemed as if everybody thought I would never succeed. I felt like seeing me struggle gave others satisfaction, even my family and teachers. It was like they were laughing at me and as if they thought I wouldn't do anything with my life.

At the same time, I knew my behavior was stressing my mom out. Since my little cousins look up to me, I knew I couldn't keep up being the way I was.

As a result, by the end of sixth grade, I didn't really get into the same amount of trouble. I would still get the not-so-pretty grades and phone calls home once in a while. Although I knew my way around to keep from getting into too much trouble, I knew I still had to take it down a couple notches because my grades were still not where I wanted them to be.

Around the beginning of seventh grade, the school counselor, Ms. Harini, suggested that we should meet twice a week. Ms. Harini wasn't like the other teachers that I had at the time. She would speak softly, and when I would talk, she would make eye contact, which showed that she really cared and that she was paying attention. Her voice was always comforting. She would tell me all the time that I'm strong enough to get through whatever I was going through.

Additionally, my grandmother had passed away two weeks before eighth grade ended. Thinking of her, I knew I didn't want to disappoint her with my grades when I got into high school. My grandmother was someone who was always poised, and I remember that she wore her hair in a bun just above her neck. Even though she had been living in Mexico, we were close, and when we were able to see each other, we'd make the best of our time together.

A few weeks before school let out for summer, people were reminiscing about all their memories and reflecting on everything that had happened to them. People were talking about how they'd changed physically, but I was realizing how much I'd also changed mentally. It occurred to me I had changed a lot compared to how I'd been in sixth grade.

During the time that I was improving myself, I also realized that before, I had been silently cutting people off. Once I stopped doing that, I was able to meet new and better people who influenced me to become a better person. To improve myself I started to become more open-minded to things and people. Before, I had been reluctant to make new friends. Now I've realized I can give people the benefit of the doubt. Sometimes I like a person's vibe, and I don't really need to talk to someone to like them as a friend.

As a result of seeing how I've changed, I've come to believe that people should take chances and see what happens, either in a positive or negative way. Anything could happen, and there are a lot of life-changing opportunities everywhere. Even if these opportunities could end up being good or bad, people should take chances.

Taking chances is the only way to learn and grow. I took chances both by being rebellious at times and by letting myself change. I need to get some of the rebellion out of my system. Something positive that I got from this is that it made me tougher. Later, by letting myself change, I learned that it does take a lot of effort to change. At times I felt like just going back to my old ways because I was so used to being that way. I'm proud that I was able to take the chance to improve myself. Even though it takes a lot of effort, I still wanted to let myself change anyway.

Taking chances is important because that's how people know what they do or don't like. They'll never know unless they try. You can learn things along the way. There are still more things I'd like to try and more chances I want to take. I want to go skydiving, go to college at either UCLA or Stanford, go to Egypt to see the pyramids, and have a pet tiger. I don't know if all these things will happen, but it's worth a try.

During seventh grade people from 826 Valencia came to my school a couple times, and I wouldn't really try. I would let the tutor speak their mind and would quietly agree with them because I really didn't want to be with just one person and try to write something. "Okay, sure, why not?" was more or less my response to everything.

Now that we're writing this essay with people from 826, I still feel a bit hesitant, but I've been trying to focus on finishing it right. I think that it's a big thing for me because, when I was younger, I would have never thought I'd actually try to write an essay with 826 or write an essay at all. It's been a long road, but I'm glad to have been through it and am looking forward to whatever comes next.

ALEJANDRA GALVAN

"I couldn't believe it. I was only in sixth grade, but it seemed like they had already given up on me."

Aaron Martinez grew up in San Francisco. He has family in El Salvador and visits there when he can. Aaron likes listening to music and playing video games. His favorite foods are quesadillas and *frijol* tamales.

WORTH WAITING FOR

BY AARON MARTINEZ

I feel great when I discover that someone is trustworthy and acting real. When I was a kid someone told me, "There are two types of friends in the world. One of them is called 'a fake friend' because they just pretend to be your friend, but later on you notice that they are out of your life. The other one is called 'a true friend' because they will always be on your side no matter what, and you will know they are real if they don't abandon you." I didn't want to believe them because I didn't want to believe some friends were fake, but I also didn't feel like they were lying to me.

Later on I learned for myself that true friends are rare. It takes work to build and grow a true friendship, and challenges can arise. It's a lot of responsibility to be a true friend. It requires inner strength to stay true to yourself and to be trustworthy.

In elementary school I used to have a group of friends. We used to hang out because we all liked to play World Wrestling Entertainment. We would pretend we were wrestlers like John Cena and Shawn Michaels and we would also play soccer with each other during PE or recess. I thought my friends were nice and that they were being themselves. I assumed they were being unique and honest. I was wrong.

During that time of my life, I learned the hard way that there are fake people around you. You have to be aware enough to see through them.

The same people I thought were being themselves started to bully me. They teased me for having an accent and not speaking "correctly." I played alone a lot and started to shut down. I felt like I didn't want to be different anymore so I stopped being me.

Before that time, I was more true to myself. I was more goofy and funny; I still am, but not as much and not as openly. I used to make jokes and laugh a lot, like I didn't have a care in the world. I didn't think as much as I do now. I was more free-spirited. After people bullied me, I stopped being myself freely. I'm more serious now. I don't feel safe being the funny guy anymore and don't trust people like I used to.

When I got sick of people bullying me, I started to bully other people to get out my anger. I had become numb; I didn't feel anything and just didn't care anymore. Then, deep down, I started to realize that it didn't feel good to treat people that way. I've since learned that people hurt each other because they feel hurt, because they've been hurt by someone else.

There were people I bullied who weren't affected by my aggression and didn't fight back. Secretly, I respected them for standing strong. They had a kind of inner strength that I appreciated.

I remember one day when I bullied a kid at school. After school I saw his mom and without thinking about it I went over to her and told her outright, "Someone is bullying your son." She went to her son and asked him who was bullying him and he pointed at me. I don't know why I did that, but I think I wanted someone to see me, so I could see myself. I also remember noticing how much his mom cared about him. Then it struck me that his mom reminded me of my mom. She was wearing a fanny pack and an SF sweater just like my mom wears. I saw myself in his shoes.

After that experience, I stopped bullying people and I said I was sorry. I feel ashamed of how I acted. I see him sometimes but we don't talk because the past still hangs between us. It is difficult to build a friendship with him now.

I went through some hard times in my younger life, like learning who my real friends are. I am now more careful about who I choose to become friends with. Here, at my high school, I'm starting to grow new friendships. I'm slowly trusting people again, and I know that building trust is a process. I think people should understand that friendship takes time to grow. It's not something you can just buy.

Real friends are loyal, supportive, trustworthy, honest, and comfortable to be around. Real friends stick with you through the hard times. It takes work to build and grow a true friendship. The kind of friend I want to be is respectful, trustworthy, and fun to be around. Friendship is the most important thing to me, next to my family. I believe that true friendships are rare and worth waiting for.

Victor Wong was born in San Francisco in 2000. He is fourteen years old, and when he is not at school he enjoys playing video games and reading history books. He particularly enjoys reading about World War II. After, school he would like to attend the University of California at Berkeley and visit Italy at some point in his life.

THOSE WHO DON'T KNOW HISTORY ARE DESTINED TO REPEAT IT

BY VICTOR WONG

My belief was not sudden and was not formed because of one event. My belief is a quote: "The farther backward you look, the farther forward you will see." Winston Churchill said this. The first time I saw the quote was on the show *Criminal Minds* two years ago. I paid attention to it because I admire Winston Churchill. Even as British cities were being reduced to rubble, he never surrendered Britain to Hitler. It is relevant to history but also to people as well. My interpretation of the quote is that history repeats itself, and we could make a change by preventing the same mistake from happening.

A point in my life that exemplifies my belief happened when I was in fourth grade and I was disorganized. I think I could say my desk looked like Abe Lincoln's office because there were papers everywhere. When I went to the next grade I was still disorganized at the start, but since I didn't want to repeat the disaster of fourth grade, I got more organized. This ties in to my belief because I learned from my past mistake, and in the end it made me a better person.

One of the examples of my belief in history is Hitler and Napoleon when they invaded Russia. In 1812 Napoleon was winning at first, but he wasn't well prepared for the Russian winter. As a result of that, many if not most of his troops froze to death or were picked off by the Russians when they retreated back to France. Hitler did a very similar thing more than a hundred years later. Like Napoleon, Hitler was winning at first in 1942 but he underestimated his opponent. The prime example of that is the battle of Stalingrad. At first the Wehrmacht, or the German military, had controlled ninety-five percent of the city, but when the winter came, the Soviets counter-attacked and eventually surrounded the Germans. Hitler ordered his general in the city, General Paulus, to not break out of the Soviet lines. Eventually the army trapped in Stalingrad ran out of supplies, and the general himself was captured on January 31, 1943. His 91,000 troops surrendered to the Soviets on February 2. After Stalingrad the Wehrmacht lost at the Battle of Kursk and soon the only city the Germans held was Leningrad. If Hitler had studied Napoleon he would not have lost and would have been more prepared.

I have made many mistakes in my own life, and I sometimes look back at them to keep them from happening again. For example, I did a project in sixth grade. I procrastinated and, well, just plain failed at it. The next year I did the project again. I procrastinated less because I didn't want to fail and I got a C-. So I guess it was a little better. I didn't realize the relevancy the quote had to the project until years later. Another event was the science fair. I did an experiment on plants and their growth. It was pretty much the same story of procrastination and laziness as the other one, the reason being I was not interested in the topic. The only difference is that my first grade was a C. I did it two years later when I was doing an experiment on dams. I did the project a week from the due date instead of a day. I got a B-, so it was a little bit better. It is hard to learn from this because it is a bad habit and I don't always realize how relevant the quote is to me. Also, this essay sort of applies to it, too— it will help me write even better. This is because it will take a few weeks to type this, to correct my vocabulary and punctuation, and to add more details.

The Russia-Ukraine Crisis, for example, is a current event in which history has repeated itself. The story of this starts in the 1990s when the Soviet Union ended and Russia and Ukraine were separate republics. The city in question was Sevastopol. Sevastopol was a major naval base for Russia. The Russians wanted to keep the city, while Ukraine wanted Russia to give them Sevastopol. The dispute was resolved by Russia giving up Sevastopol to Ukraine, and Ukraine leasing Russia some of its naval bases. But very recently, the Ukrainian president Viktor Yanukovych was removed from power. This outraged many of the Russians in Ukraine, and they protested. Russia sent in their military to help resolve the crisis. They annexed the region of Crimea, where the city of Sevastopol was located. If the Ukraine had looked back in history they possibly would have been more prepared by building their navy or splitting up the region into a Russian and Ukrainian side because they would have known Russia still wanted the area.

The Korean (1950–1953) and Vietnam (1967–1975) wars are another example of when people have not learned from history. These wars are similar in how they were set up. Both of them had a communist north and a democratic south. The United States fought in the two wars but there were two different outcomes. In the Korean War the United States, which came in to Korea as the UN (United Nations) forces, was winning at first. Only the Chinese army, which outnumbered them, pushed them back until eventually an armistice was signed dividing Korea along the 38th parallel. This action prevented another world war from happening. In the Vietnam War it was difficult to fight a war because the North Vietnamese Army (NVA) and their civilian counterpart, the Viet Cong, were fighting a guerrilla war against the U.S. This was one of the reasons the war dragged on for a long time until public support for it waned. If the U.S. would have negotiated with the Vietnamese as it had in the Korean War, there would have been a decisive ending and a better outcome for both sides.

Just like people in history, I sometimes have not learned from my past mistakes. Ever since sixth grade I have done my homework in class before, instead at home. Well, this obviously affected my grades because sometimes I couldn't finish it in time. So my middle school grades were not as good as they are in high school right now. Even now I still do that from time to time and it has become a bad habit.

The League of Nations and the UN again provide evidence of people learning from history. After the First World War, the League of Nations was created to stop another one from happening, and, as many people know, it failed. It had no real authority or power, and it also lacked an army. The Great Powers—the U.S., Soviet Union, Britain, and China—were supposed to provide an army but when they refused to do so, well, the League was powerless. Also, many countries never joined the League or had very short memberships. The decision-making process was very slow. The League of Nations lasted until it was effectively disbanded and replaced by the UN in 1945. After World War II the Great Powers analyzed what the League did wrong, and that was how the UN was created. The Security Council was a new feature added in the UN that was different from the League. These countries are granted extra power and can veto things from the main council. Because they analyzed what they did wrong, they prevented a third world war from happening.

My belief matters because most people and the world have usually analyzed and looked at their mistakes, and when they didn't, well, there were consequences—like Hitler and Napoleon, Korea and Vietnam, and maybe even both World Wars. When they did look back they did better, like the League of Nations and the UN. The same mistake was not repeated. This has also applied to me with my projects and my homework when I did or did not learn from my mistakes. This belief can apply to history and to ordinary people too.

Alejandro Colindres was born and raised in San Francisco. He is fifteen years old and is currently enrolled at Mission High School. He enjoys eating sushi, drawing, hanging out with friends, and playing video games. His superpower of choice would be invincibility, but he would still choose to die of old age. If he were an animal, he would be a house cat, because he likes being inside.

HERE COMES TROUBLE

BY ALEJANDRO COLINDRES

I believe that trouble is a lesson in disguise. As adults and children we can all agree that we've gotten in a lot of trouble before. This creates fear of what punishments await. What children never seem to see is that they are getting yelled at to teach them lessons about what is right, what is wrong, caution, mindfulness, frugality, hard work, and acceptance.

It was a warm fall afternoon and I had just gotten back from school. I was relaxing on my couch when my parents boomed through the doorway, like the Heavy from Team Fortress 2, asking if I'd finished my assignments. I told them as usual that I had finished them. This was, of course, a lie. Around this time I'd become very fond of playing video games on my computer. Playing Team Fortress 2 was more important to me than doing my schoolwork. I began to fail.

My parents noticed that my grades were plummeting. When they saw that, they were so mad I thought they were going do me in like the heavy-weapons guy in my game. They told me that I had to fix my act. I was sweating and shaking because sometimes my parents get very disappointed with how I behave in school. They later called my teacher, and my teacher told my mother that I was "a bright and intelligent student" and that he had faith in me. After that time I've always tried my best on any assignment I have due. I do this because I want to get good grades to prove that I really am "a bright and intelligent student." From this, I learned that my parents had yelled at me and called my teacher to teach me a lesson of hard work and responsibility. My parents care very deeply about education. They think that knowledge is the key to success and power because they both didn't get the same opportunities as me. They don't want me to make the same mistakes they did.

It was a hot late-summer day, and I was attending an after-school program at my middle school. It seemed like any other day. I was talking to some friends and we all agreed that we should just not go to the after-school program and instead go to the corner store to grab some snacks. So we all grabbed our stuff and went up the hill toward the corner store. We got our snacks and decided to just go back to school and eat our chips and sodas. This is where we went wrong.

When we came back, an instructor caught us red-handed back on campus with food in our hands. She took us to the main hallway where we waited for our parents. The main hallway was a frigid place where all the passersby watched us sitting in shame, on the nippy benches and on the frozen steps. I was panicking at this time, frantic with fear of my parents scolding me. I decided to give my Funyuns to my friend to rid myself of possible "evidence." It felt like ages as I waited in the sheer cold of that hallway.

My dad came to pick me up as he always did but when he came he didn't ask any questions. Instead he showed me love. My parents told me that they weren't mad at me. Rather, they were concerned for my well-being. This meant that I gave away my Funyuns for no reason! My parents said to be careful when out on the streets. They told me that the reason why they took us to the main hall was to keep an eye out for us so that we wouldn't leave campus again. My parents told me that if I were to leave the campus and get hurt,

ALEJANDRO COLINDRES

the after-school coordinators wouldn't be able to help me because I wouldn't be under their supervision. I haven't done anything like that again because I don't enjoy going to corner stores. I wouldn't want to go against my parents' instructions. The lesson I learned was not to stray from groups and to be mindful of my surroundings because my parents value my well-being and my safety.

If society were to agree entirely with my belief, there would be a large amount of optimism. A lot of people would see that every decision they make has a positive consequence. Good can come out of bad choices when you take the time to acknowledge your mistakes and see what changes you can make to the future. When someone gets mad at you for your bad choices, their punishment should encourage you to realize your errors and learn. For example, my parents get mad at me a lot and it's because they love me. I think that they do this because they are concerned for my well-being. By following this belief, I've come to understand that after all these years, all my parents have done is teach me how to better myself. They did this through lessons including responsibility, hard work, caution, and inclusiveness. I believe that trouble is a lesson in disguise.

Desjone Fisher, who is known as DJ, was born in San Mateo, California, and has been living in San Francisco her whole life. She enjoys playing basketball, hanging out with friends at the mall, and spending time at the salon while getting massages with her mom. DJ believes that hard work pays off. She is currently learning Mandarin in a Chinese-language class and believes that if she works hard through school it will lead to a good career and lifestyle.

THE DAY I INJURED MY ANKLE WAS THE DAY I CHANGED

BY DESJONE FISHER

In the melting heat of the summer of 2012, between sixth and seventh grade, I was playing basketball and got injured for the first time. My friend and I were playing inside a San Francisco State University gym against four grown-ups. I was working up a sweat, and it smelled like a stinky gorilla was inside the gym because everyone else was sweating too. My friend passed me the ball at the top of the three-pointer. I cautiously dribbled the ball with my right hand, ran to the basket to make a layup, but then the tallest grown-up guarded me. I took a step back to get a better shot, but then my ankle snapped. It felt like my leg was on fire and a bunch of venomous spiders had just bit my leg. I instantly fell to the ground with a loud thud and started to roll around. The grown-ups told me to stop moving, so I did, and they realized that I was crying. They asked me to take a deep breath. Then they picked me up and called my mom to tell her what happened.

After my injury, my mom and the doctor both said that I had to rest my ankle and take it easy from basketball. I couldn't play for six weeks. After I discovered this news, I felt very bitter and irritated that I couldn't play basketball for a while. I became very bored at home, with no one there but my dogs.

At home with my injured ankle, I decided to conduct research on basketball to better understand the rules of the game and how to take care of a basketball injury. I searched the Internet for two to three hours each day, watching the greatest basketball replays, understanding what not to do in basketball, and learning how many fouls the average player got in a game. I also studied games on TV and saw how the greatest of greats played ball, many of whom are my favorite players, like Lebron James (aka King James), Michael Jordan, Stephen Curry, and Dwyane Wade. I also watched college ball, like my favorite women's team from the University of Connecticut. This is how I started to change my own game—partly because I didn't want to hurt my ankle again. I decided for myself that I needed to change so that I could be a better player. I also wanted to be more careful the next time I played, so I wouldn't hurt myself again.

While I was healing, I snuck out to do basic drills like dribbling up and down the court, passing behind my back, and dribbling between my legs. My mom and I would go on two-mile runs. With all the limping I was doing, I'm sure I looked like a galloping horse. Over time my ankle became stronger.

My shooting form needed to be improved. I decided to start focusing on my shooting hand by making it look like I was keeping my hand "in the cookie jar" after the ball left my hand. I consistently made the ball into the basket. It touched nothing but net and it made that sweet snapping sound, like someone had just snapped the world's largest Kit Kat bar in half. With all this practice, I improved. I also learned that in order to be a better player I had to respect the rules, not only the rules of basketball but in school too.

I was in kindergarten when I first started playing. Back then, I didn't have to work so hard in school to play basketball. Up until my injury

I used to be a big procrastinator in school, doing my homework right before the assignment was due. Sometimes I never even completed my work. When I hurt my ankle, I realized that basketball has such an impact on my life. When my ankle healed, I began to believe that I needed to get good grades in order to keep playing basketball. I stepped up my academic game by working hard in school and getting my work done on time.

These days, I finish my classwork to ask the teacher questions so that I can better understand the homework. When I don't complete my work at school, I actually bring my work home to finish. Bad grades were once a burden. I felt like the Hunchback of Notre Dame, I had so much weight on my shoulders. Now that I get good grades, I want to share the good news with my parents. It's hard for me to work harder, but I'm proud of myself right now. Even now that I take a Chinese class I struggle with all the work, but I've pushed myself and did my best to turn in all my homework for that class. I now have an A in that class, but that does not mean that I get to slack off just because I have a good grade. I still have to work hard to keep that A. I changed for myself and decided to get better grades in school so I didn't have to worry about not being able to play. I changed and continue to change to the best of my abilities.

After I decided to change for basketball, everything else in my life changed, like working hard in school, eating healthy, and changing the way I worked out. This change has helped me look to the future; the experience has helped steer me onto the path to believe that I can make it into the WNBA. If not that career, then I also have a goal to become an engineer. I wouldn't be as driven as I am now if I didn't believe that change starts with me.

Riley Coltrane Clark is a center-mid striker who has roughly one hundred thousand freckles on his left arm. Riley enjoys playing soccer, dreaming about his future law career, listening to music, and traveling (physically and mentally). He speaks fluent Spanish and would like one 3 x 3, one Neapolitan milkshake, and Animal Fries, please.

IN FRONT OF A GIANT WALL

BY RILEY CLARK

Unhappiness is like being in front of a giant wall; all you see is hardship in front of you, not what's on the other side of your feelings. If a person is too caught up in their own gloom, they're too distracted to get anything done. I can personally relate to this. In my life, vast distances and separation have occurred with my family and friends, but I chose not to be too melancholy about it because I knew I would see them again. These encounters prepared me for my future and taught me that life goes on.

Kelton was born in Portland, Oregon, and lived in Mazatlan, Mexico at the same time that my family did. We met Kelton at a basketball game where his dad, who towers over everyone like a skyscraper, was screaming at him in English. That caught our attention not only because of his height, but also because he was one of the few people not speaking Spanish. We approached Kelton, talked to him a little, and went our separate ways. Later that week, close to my birthday, my dad ran into Kelton's dad and invited Kelton to my birthday party. If our dads were not in the exact place they were, we wouldn't have befriended Kelton.

Kelton was a key piece in my life in Mexico and he still is. When we moved back to the United States it was halfway through the fifth grade, and he felt like we ditched him. Kelton and I both had to realize that we didn't live in the same city and that we couldn't hang out anymore. Living in Mexico as a small child, I made many friends and lost touch with all of them, except Kelton. We text each other every day and even with the distance we are still best friends.

Someone who also shares my belief that life goes on is my mom. When I was little my mom was a videographer for many big music groups like Michael Jackson, the Eagles, and Gloria Estefan. She was on tour for four to six months at a time. Not everything was bad about my mom working for so long, though. While she was gone, my dad gave us more privileges than we usually had. He let us eat candy and drink soda, something my mother would never let us do. Even though we had more Skittles and Coca-Cola while she was gone, I still missed her tucking me in at night. We had to continue with life while she was gone. We talked almost every night on the phone, and she sent us postcards from all over the country, and whenever we were lucky enough to see her on the road we took the opportunity.

It was a hot day somewhere in Arizona. The only things my dad, my brother, and I could see were a fence, an ocean of sand, and a stadium or concert hall. We were visiting my mom at an Eagles concert. I remember being able to smell the buttery popcorn all the way from the parking lot and hearing the electrified screams of the fans. From a distance we saw a small figure coming toward us. As the silhouette grew closer we realized it was our mom. We recognized her not only because of her standard work attire—she wore all-black clothes so that she wouldn't be seen by the cameras, and a press pass—but also her blonde hair and height. We started climbing the fence into the parking lot toward her. We immediately started running. When we reached her, we were ecstatic and jumped into her arms. In the short time that

I saw my mom that day, we left the concert feeling better and I understood that life goes on.

I'm more prepared for the future now, because I've gone through separation and sadness, like not having a mom for a while and my best friend living in another country. I will be faced with more lugubrious feelings and I will view them differently after already facing challenges. I won't let sorrow consume my life. I will climb over the wall that separates my feelings from reality.

Khier Viray was born in Manila, Philippines, but he immigrated to San Francisco in 2007. He has some fancy dribbling skills, which come in handy, since he likes playing point guard with his old middle school crew. If you want to be his friend, feel free to bring him his favorite food, cheese pizza.

STRUGGLING? THAT'S COOL.

BY KHIER VIRAY

It started in middle school, when I was a lazy boy. I was lazy like that feeling when you wake up in the morning on a school day and you're tired as heck, and just want to go back to bed. I also used to just play video games, eat, and chill out with my friends. In eighth grade my friend Abhishek and I planned to play basketball every day after school. But the problem was, I got lazy and I didn't want to go. My friend Abhishek started preaching about hard work. He said I was passive, and I always stayed home playing video games. I got frustrated after a while because he was lecturing me. It's not right because he's younger than me. Plus, I also don't like being lectured.

The day after Abhishek lectured me, I was at home, chilling on the couch and thinking about what Abhishek said to me. He made me feel like I was a loser. In my mind, though, I thought, "I think he's kind of right." I felt embarrassed because he proved me wrong.

I went up to him the next day and said, "Hey, I think I'm ready."

He said, "What do you mean?"

"To put in hard work."

He said, "All right, that's the Khier Viray I know."

The next day, after school, he introduced me to the basketball coaches. I was nervous because I thought they were going to ask me many questions, but they just asked me how badly I wanted to be on the team. I was so nervous I didn't say anything; I just nodded and smiled.

In the weeks after he introduced me to the basketball coaches, Abhishek and I always played basketball after school, even though we were always as hungry as tigers when school let out. It was cool, though. I started enjoying and getting used to the running and the drills. I even lost weight. The week after, Abhishek mentioned that tryouts for the basketball team were after school. So, I went to the tryouts, and the basketball court was packed. My thoughts were moving as fast as a Lamborghini because all the other kids were intimidating. They were looking at me to see I how played. We ran a couple of suicide sprints, but we mostly did scrimmages, and I did well. I made a couple of three-pointers. I crossed this one dude named Jaraughn, and I made him think that I was dribbling right, but I actually went left.

When tryouts ended, the coaches announced who made the team and my whole body started shaking like I was shivering in the cold. I thought I was going to get cut from the team. But hey, guess what? I made it onto the basketball team. I felt proud of myself, and all my friends were happy. My friends and I decided to celebrate by going to McDonald's and eating McDoubles, fries, and drinking Coke, just simple food. I didn't want to eat a lot, especially after I played basketball.

The best part is I proved wrong all the haters who doubted me. I have to have love for my friends, though, because they were there for me all the time and supported me. They're the reason why I'm not so lazy anymore. One thing that I learned from this is the belief that if you put all your heart into something you really love or like, it will eventually pay off. All of the hard work that I put into making the basketball team—it was all worth it.

If you have a friend like Abhishek who's always there for you when you need him, and always supports you through the struggle that you're going through, make sure to follow and respect that friend. One more thing: if you're struggling with sports or school stressors— and I'm talking to all the people who are going through the same thing that I did—just believe in yourself and don't worry or care about what other people think of you. They're just there to distract you; in life there's always that one person who's trying to ruin your dreams. As I said earlier, just put all your heart into something you love or like, and the hard work will eventually pay off.

David Garcia is from the Mission District in San Francisco. He's fourteen years old, and he has a younger brother. He likes history and he plays baseball (he prefers center field, but he'll play first base too). David thinks that writing, even when it's fiction, is usually about the truth.

NEW SCHOOL, OLD SCRIPT

BY DAVID GARCIA

I liked my middle school. I liked my teachers, I liked how diverse it was, and I had good friends. The day I graduated from middle school I said goodbye to friends and teachers, took some pictures, and went home. I got on my video game console and then my friends got on and we played all night. That was one of best moments of my life. Each one of my friends was online that night, and in that moment I forgot that I wasn't going to be able to see them soon. We were all different, and that's what made our group complete.

We were a group of five: Jorge played soccer and was the one who cracked jokes, Erik would always be in trouble and he would rage at the video game we played, Alex was a party animal who would always play video games with me and was my best friend, Peter was the cool guy who would barely play video games and loved his beats. Me? I was the quiet guy who played video games every day and would barely talk in class. We each defined our own life and wrote our own script—we could be ourselves around each other.

A few weeks after I graduated, my mom and dad told me that I would go to the Mission High School summer program. And then they told me that I could pick the high school I wanted to go to if I didn't like Mission. I didn't want to go to Mission High School but I knew that I had to. That meant that I wouldn't see my friends and my baseball coach, and that made me so upset. For the first month at Mission I still kept in touch with my friends, but after the first semester we didn't talk to each other anymore. At first I thought it was my fault. Then I thought maybe it was my parents I should be blaming, not myself, but it wasn't just them.

Later in the year I just didn't care anymore. Leaving my friends behind was like being the only person on earth. I was alone without my friends. It took me a long time to realize that baseball season wasn't that far away and I would be able to see my old friends then.

The only thing I was worried about was making friends. The first friends I made at Mission were all troublemakers. At first it looked like they were different, like my old friends, because they didn't let people tell them what to do. They really didn't let people write their script. They would do whatever they wanted. I was sitting at their table one day and my friends got in trouble for talking a lot and not doing work. I remember the teacher calling my name really loudly. Then he called me over to his desk and told me to stay after class. That's when I realized I had to pick some different friends. My troublemaker friends were using my belief, which is that you define your own life, as an excuse to do whatever they wanted. I had hoped that they would use the belief to stay true to themselves.

It's been a while since this happened, but whenever I watch a movie I notice that my belief is common in a lot of storytelling. In superhero movies, the superhero gets hated on and everyone tells him to act like a normal human. And then, usually in a big standoff with a bad guy, the superhero acts bravely and chooses how he wants to define his own life. He saves the day and everybody loves him for choosing who he wants to be.

This kind of storytelling sometimes happens in real life; that's the reason we like these stories so much. We believe it's possible to be

DAVID GARCIA

who we want to be. Someone in my life who shares my belief is my uncle, because when he was my age, he would get in a lot of trouble all the time. He would get in fights and not do his homework. Then he dropped out of high school because he didn't like people bossing him around. After going his own path he's now the head chef of a restaurant. He has always worked hard and made his own decisions. Both stories, in comics and in real life, make me think about what's possible in the future.

Kim Perez was born in Mexico City and has lived all over North America, from snowy Toronto to sunny San Francisco, which she now calls home. Kim likes sleeping late and listening to music, but finds having too much homework annoying. If she had three wishes, she would make sure her mom stayed healthy, see a lot of great lands, and be able to shoot pizza out of her hands.

BELIEVE
IN YOURSELF

BY KIM PEREZ

Believe in yourself, even when no one else does. I've seen my family believing in themselves even though their own family members discouraged them. My parents' dream was to live in Canada. They believed that if they moved to Canada with their daughters and worked really hard to make their dream come true, they could start a new life. My dad's parents said that his dream was impossible and that he needed a miracle to make it come true. My dad felt very disappointed when his parents said that. My mom trusted my dad, and they both were so sure about moving to another country. After two years of fifteen-hour workdays seven days a week, their dream came true.

I learned this belief for myself in middle school when my teachers told me I was going to repeat eighth grade. One day, I was waiting with my mom for the school bell to ring outside. Then I saw one of my teachers, Ms. H. She told my mom that I should get my homework done and go to sleep early, because those habits were affecting the chances of me going to high school. My mom gave me a look and said, "Don't worry, Ms. H, I'll make sure that she gets all her homework done." When Ms. H left, my mom told me that we were going to have a talk after school. I felt terrified because my mom said that we needed to talk, but I was frustrated because Ms. H had told my mom about my bad habits in school. Before I started believing in my belief, I was very negative. I used to fall asleep during class, and I wouldn't get my homework done. When my parents talked to me about my grades and how I ditched some of my classes, I felt nervous and scared because I didn't know what their reaction would be after the principal told them I had been ditching classes by hiding in the school bathrooms. I thought my parents would be disappointed in me, because they thought I was a "nice girl." They didn't know I would go so far as to ditch class. But after my teacher said that I wasn't going to pass eighth grade, I felt dejected and disappointed, and that's when I had to start believing in myself.

After I graduated from middle school, I thought high school would be more important; I would have to change my bad habits. I stopped sleeping in class and started to get my homework done. Now that I'm in high school I feel different and more positive. Conceptual physics is one of my favorite classes because it's interesting and I learn new things every day. For example, I always thought that the sky was blue, but in reality the sky is black. When I found out that the sky was black I felt disappointed but also engaged. I think it's a fun class because we get to choose our own groups when we do important projects. I do extra-credit homework to try to keep my grades up. Teachers treat me differently because, even though I'm not a perfect student, I finish my work. And I even received a student-of-the-month award. My teachers don't see me as a bad student, and I don't have a bad image anymore.

When I was in middle school I had a friend who always was saying that nobody believed in her and that she was worthless. She believed this because she wanted to go out with a girl, and she told me that she also felt that way because she didn't feel support or love from her parents. I told her that she had me by her side, and that she shouldn't worry about her negative parents. Instead she should start to believe in herself. She had hope about her parents accepting her relationship. After a while, she forgave her parents, and even though her parents didn't support her, she never gave up and never stopped believing in herself. At first she felt worthless, but when she started to believe in herself she looked so happy. She used to be disrespectful, but now she's relaxed and respects others. She is even more friendly.

Now that I started to believe in myself everything has changed for me. I get good grades and I feel happy when my parents tell me that they feel proud and not disappointed. I feel more successful. Sometimes I still get scared of making the same mistake and stop believing in myself. If I don't want that to happen, I should never stop believing in myself because that's the only thing that is going to help me reach my goals. I don't have a real picture of what I want to do with my life yet, but I'm pretty sure that I want to go to college. My belief will help me reach my goal.

Deyring Toruno was born in San Francisco on the first day of the new millenium: January 1, 2000. He likes football, super burritos, and pancakes with bananas. If he could have any superpower, Deyring would choose flying because it sure beats taking the bus. The real-life power he values most is determination, which has helped him stay positive and succeed in school.

THE HARD-PUNCHING REPORT CARD

BY DEYRING TORUNO

Coming home tired from a busy day of school, I walked up the steps and saw my mom with a slip of paper that said SFUSD. I knew it was my report card. I tried to play it off and go to my room to change. But she stopped me before I left. She gave me a mean look; I felt the guilt and I didn't even know what my GPA was. My mom handed me the slip, and I was shocked about how low it was: a 1.36 GPA. I knew I didn't do all the work but I didn't know it was going to come out that badly. She started talking to me and kept saying how she wasn't mad, but disappointed. She kept going on about how she wanted me to be successful because I got a free education, and that I was not taking advantage of it. I could see a tear shedding from her eye. I had never realized how much my mom cared about my education. I spent the rest of the day in my room surrounded by my posters of athletes and Ninja Turtles, lying down and thinking of how proud I could make my parents. I felt like it was an obligation for me to do something about this.

While I was lying down, I looked at my poster and thought of a belief I had. My belief is that with determination you will succeed. This belief was kind of inspired by loving the sport of boxing. As a kid I was always into boxing. My stepdad wanted to show my older brother how to box because he was a little overweight. Just looking at them, I would always try to join in, even being a little annoying sometimes. I would stand in the corner and shadowbox on my own, imitating what my big brother would do. A few months later I got a gift: my very own boxing gloves. The gloves were all red with a gold velcro strap saying EVERLAST, with my name on the thumb of the glove printed in gold. They said they would let me train with them now. It could be sparring with my brother or punching the bag for one hour. I knew it was something I loved and something that I would never stop doing.

Going through the years I would love to watch fights with my family and this one guy caught my attention with his dedication. A role model. The one and only Floyd Mayweather. He would always bring up these little quotes or statements on his show, called 24/7, that I found out about through loving the sport. The quote that stuck with me was, "With determination you will succeed."

Before believing in this, I was just a regular kid who played sports, struggled in school, and didn't do anything about it. I just could not stop getting distracted in school. I felt horrible for my parents, knowing that they had higher expectations for me. They wanted me to be the first one in my family to attend college, so I have made that my main goal ever since.

My dad and stepdad were two main people that helped and supported me to form my belief. Both of them at different times would have meaningful talks with me about how I should be doing better in school. They said if you work hard, you will succeed. It was pretty easy to believe this, but I knew it was going to be hard to put it into action.

So the next morning after I got my bad report card, I went to shower and my morning alarm went off. It was pretty, loud like a baby crying. My mom woke up and sarcastically said, "If only you had an alarm for your homework." I was not sure if she was kidding or not. So after I changed in my room, I had some spare time, and I actually ended up putting an alarm for every weekday at 7:30 to do homework. Coming home after school I would be in my room and my phone would start vibrating at 7:30 p.m. My mom just looked at me, kind of surprised at seeing me doing my homework at a certain time with her not even knowing about the alarm. So the first week of the new marking period was a breeze. But the next two weeks I started getting super lazy and not finishing the homework until the next morning or a few minutes before it was due.

While I was falling behind and struggling, all I would think about were my parents. I had a flashback to when I was working with my stepdad, and all he had to do was paint a white trim around a window. It took him thirty minutes to paint the small window. I asked him, "Why take so long on something so small?" He said, "It doesn't matter if it's big or small, you put in effort to make it look good." I automatically thought that he was referring to me.

I feel like everyone in the world should believe in this. It can be the inspiration or motivation to a success in their life. It will make people realize how they can be successful if they do put the time and determination into it. And with more successful people in the world, it would make a huge difference. Imagine how many people have hidden talents or specialties in the world, but now they can't do anything because they didn't put the effort into it when they had the chance. The world would be more futuristic right now if everyone in life was successful, because maybe with all the inventions people might have thought of, they could've possibly changed the world.

"I would stand in the corner and shadowbox on my own, imitating what my big brother would do. A few months later I got a gift: my very own boxing gloves."

Working hard through the marking period, I had a gut feeling that I was going to do well. Grades were coming in soon, and I was anxiously waiting for the report card to come. It was like my birthday, and I was waiting for my presents. At around 2 P.M., the mailman passed by and I blazed to the mailbox. I brought the report card back upstairs and also called in my brother to check it out with me. My mom was not home, and I was just wondering what she was going to say. I heard her coming up the steps with my stepdad.

She came in and instantly saw the report card on the coffee table in the living room. I handed it to her, looking into her eyes with my puppy eyes. You could see the disappointment in her face as soon as I gave her the card. She then opened it, and immediately rushed toward me and congratulated me. My stepdad seemed confused, so he picked up the report card and also saw the GPA I had. I had accomplished getting a 3.86. I felt like it was a huge weight lifted off my back. Coming from failing and having a 1.36 GPA to a 3.86 showed me that I was capable of getting top-notch grades. It made me realize how these little things, like doing homework or seeing my teacher for five minutes during lunch, can really make a huge difference. It really made me and my family happy. So from then on I have believed in that belief, and I am still on that journey to be the first in my family to go to college. I know I will accomplish that goal because "with determination you will succeed."

Emajae Hackett was born in Oakland and has lived all throughout the Bay Area. She understands and values her heritage, which is why she loves her Ethnic Studies class. In addition to having an amazing, bright mind, Emajae is a true creative soul. Many of her friends would be surprised to find out that she enjoys poetry. Coming from a unique family environment, Emajae considers her mother her best friend, values lessons her dad has taught her, and remains close to her siblings despite living in different households. Emajae is conquering her fear of failing by planning a life full of goals and dreams.

INNER LOVE

BY EMAJAE HACKETT

In the beginning of seventh grade, I met this boy named Erick. He was very loving and treated me kindly. I was infatuated with him. I was excited and happy when he asked me to be his girlfriend. Erick and I never argued in the beginning. We were always together; if you saw him, you would see me. Eight months passed, and something about him changed when his father got shot in East Oakland for no reason. His father's passing really took a toll on Erick. I knew what he was going through not having a father around, because my father was in jail most of my life. But whenever I tried to comfort him, he would start to yell at me and call me names. He would say, "Leave me alone," and call me a mean name. I felt offended. I wasn't expecting someone that I loved to disrespect me. But I let it happen because I felt like it was okay; it's a part of loving someone. I wanted to be there for him when he needed someone the most.

But he resented me for his father's death due to all the time we spent together. He felt that it was time that could have been spent with his father. But it wasn't like we were always together on purpose. We went to the same school, so we would see each other in the halls and at PE. After school we would take the same buses because he always went to his grandmother's house. His grandmother lived right next to me and that's why we spent most of our time together. But after his father passed, he wasn't with me as much. He started to stay at school longer with his friends instead of getting on the same bus. We started arguing a lot about spending time with each other because for me, it wasn't enough. Even though we went to the same school, we only saw each other one day of the week. I felt like he was running away from me. Two months later, he broke up with me. I was heartbroken. I felt like I'd been burned but my heart was ice cold, like Elsa from *Frozen,* who couldn't be free. This affected my schoolwork as well. My GPA fell from a 3.5 to a 2.9.

I never really told anyone about my breakup, because I was embarrassed to tell people how my relationship was going downhill while all my friends' relationships seemed fine. But thank God I had my mom by my side. She always knew the truth and when she knew something was up, then it needed to be fixed. She always said that Erick wasn't any good for me, but I never listened. She advised me not to put my all into him. People said that I was too young to love, but I knew what love was because I experienced love with my family and knew how it felt. But when we were going out, I started losing focus on what was important to me—which was myself! I put all my attention toward him, and ended up loving him more than myself until he really hurt my feelings and said that he didn't want to be with me anymore.

It was hard for me because I was used to being with him. So it was difficult to change my routine since he was always a part of it. My heart was aching, but I couldn't let it be broken anymore. I had to start loving myself. After our breakup, I had time to think about things more. Constantly being around one person and not giving them space can be annoying because sometimes you need to be away from them to realize how much you don't need them. I learned that you really have to love yourself before you love someone else. If you don't, your emotions will get hurt and you'll feel empty inside because all the love you give is given to someone else who doesn't deserve it. At that time, he needed to love himself as well, and wasn't ready to receive the love he was given.

I began writing my feelings down. I also started to listen to music, which helped me cry and get my feelings out until I didn't hurt anymore. My music went from sad and depressing to "get-over-him-you-deserve-better" type music. My favorite sad song to listen to was Tynisha Keli's "I Wished You Loved Me." My favorite get-over-him song was Fantasia's "Free Yourself."

After a while, my heart started to go back to its natural form—where I could love again. As my heart healed, I began to love myself and others by focusing equally on that person and myself.

Seventh grade was kind of a roller coaster. There were good times and there were some bad ones. But I overcame this hardship in my life by loving myself and knowing that I deserved more than what I was receiving. Now that I put my belief into action, I have a wonderful boyfriend, and we've been together for one year now.

By the way, my GPA is a 3.6.

Esly Juarez is a fourteen-year-old ninth grader from San Francisco. He most enjoys sleeping and playing sports. Esly sincerely enjoys the movie *8 Mile* and has dreams of traveling to Europe. For Esly, his English class has become an expressive outlet that he enjoys.

LIGHT AT THE END OF THE TUNNEL

BY ESLY JUAREZ

I always think that a new chance could be the light at the end of a dark tunnel.

I believe in second chances because I remain idealistic about the future. I think that exposure to second chances can help bth the person giving the second chance, and the person receiving the second chance to mature in their own right. A part of remaining confident in the future and maturing is putting your differences aside for a better cause, giving and getting forgiveness, and being optimistic.

Second chances are important because it gives you an opportunity to put your differences aside for a better cause. This knowledge comes from personal experience. I was in a situation with my cousin regarding one of his friends. The guy was constantly irritating me, the way my alarm clock does when the loud Rap God song goes off in the morning. For example, he proclaimed himself the leader and would demand things from us. He would often make derogatory, underhanded remarks to me and to the rest of the group. But due to their two-of-a-kind relationship, I noticed he was a valued companion to my cousin. Therefore, as a group we decided to give him a second chance, allowing us to put our differences aside for a better cause. As a result, this helped me mature and increased my tolerance to interact with different characters in life.

Experience also gives me the idea that forgiveness is an important part of giving second chances. Last year around the end of the school year, during class, a friend of mine shockingly kicked me in the genitals, as if they were soccer balls. He got mad after an incident where we were wrestling and during the go-to-sleep maneuver, he missed his spot and botched the whole move. After his head smashed into my knee, he quickly fell to the floor. Shortly thereafter I helped him off the floor by scraping his skinny body off the pavement. I placed his body on a lunch bench. After the second he had to breathe, I saw him walking toward me with anger in his eyebrows. It was then that he decided to get vengeance on me.

Following that incident I thought about whether I really needed a friend with a quick-trigger temper. I decided to forgive him because he was funny, relaxed, and charismatic. I matured in my own right from this experience by learning not to cry over spilled milk.

Optimism plays a strong factor in giving second chances. A clear example of this is in the movie *8 Mile*. In the movie, Grammy Award-winning rapper Eminem's character Jimmy "B-Rabbit" Smith is pushed by his crew of friends and his new girlfriend. They encourage him to keep rap battling, remaining optimistic that Jimmy possessed the skill of rapping even though the last time he rapped competitively, he lost by way of cold feet.

I can personally connect to this because at one point my mom was having a midlife crisis after losing her job due to injury, causing her to fall into a state of depression, excessive sleeping, and moodiness. Remaining optimistic that she would pull through, I gave her many chances by accepting what she was going through and realizing that she would hop back on her two feet. Giving her those second chances helped me mature by witnessing firsthand the downfall of a hardworking mother and a loving wife. Seeing this made me realize the amount of power the human body and mind possess. This helped me remain idealistic about the future because I had faith that she would get back on her feet, and it would lead us to restore our relationship.

Second chances are a major factor within life because they give you the opportunity to reflect on whether you made the right decision. If you're giving someone a second chance, you get a feeling of being mature and the bigger person. If you're receiving the second chance, you get a sense of love and the feeling of care that someone would forgive you for a mistake. I know it's hard to give second chances, but it's even harder to live with wondering if your future would have been different if you had gotten a second chance at an important moment. At the end of the day I think the light at the end of the dark tunnel is the second chance at the end of a dark journey.

Isaac Alvarez was born and raised in San Francisco. He is a student at Mission High School. He loves soccer and is excited to be attending the San Jose Earthquakes Soccer Academy this summer. He enjoys music and intends to practice piano and guitar.

CHANGE COMES FROM WITHIN

BY ISAAC ALVAREZ

When life came at me sideways and everything was getting difficult, I didn't do much to make the change I needed. I was overwhelmed and was just waiting for someone to come into my life and change things for me. I had the idea that there was nothing I could do. Around the end of my seventh grade year, I started changing things completely around. I went from not going to school at all to actually going. I also started making better decisions outside of school and started helping out more around my home. A big reason I was able to change was because I learned that I could change things myself. I realized that no one was going to come and change things for me and that if I wanted to transform my life, I was going to have to dedicate myself to it.

Even before I started to change, I got help from a handful of people—family, friends, and teachers—who helped me with little things, from supportive words to taking me out to eat. These things made me relax and take a breath.

I remember one time in my seventh grade year I had a court hearing for truancy. The judges at the hearing really put an ear out for what I had to say. They understood my situation and told me they would give me some time to get my things together, before they got out of control. They said the situation could escalate to the point where I'd have to get put in a foster home, but even that didn't change much in my mind. This wasn't enough to make the change in my mindset, unfortunately.

My home situation was as complicated as an unsolved Rubik's Cube, and this made school as important as last year's news. My absolutely atrocious attendance was something I needed to change; I knew it myself at the time but I never had the mindset to try to change it myself. The mind-set I had at the time was passive; I didn't really care about what was happening, I thought I couldn't do anything to make the change I needed.

Changing things slowly was hard, but one day I woke up and everything was completely different, or at least that's how it felt. I decided from that day forward to take responsibility for what I could, for myself. I put my newfound belief into action that day.

I soon started taking responsibility for myself and my actions. I slowly started changing everything in my life, from improving my attendance in school to trying to help out as much as I could at home. I also fell in love with the game of *fútbol*; that was one of the things that kept me going. I've been playing it my whole life, but all of a sudden it felt like I was addicted to the sport. I started seeing how *fútbol* is a path toward a better, positive future. I will follow that path to make it happen, through self-motivation and dedication.

Making a change isn't always fun, and motivating yourself isn't always easy. Sometimes you find yourself confronting unexpected challenges out in the world and also within yourself.

One night there I was, at one in the morning, doing my daily training routine. I was really putting my belief in action. I thought to myself, *What are you doing here at one in the morning?* I was pushing myself— I had been there since eleven, trying to put in more effort, more time for myself. After running the stairs at City College time after time,

I stopped and asked myself what I was doing there. It was getting cold; the people who were here earlier had left a while ago. It was extremely foggy and I was tired.

I was practicing my footwork at the time. I stopped to take a breath and when I looked back, a spear full of fear struck me. In the shadows I saw a dark figure out of the corner of my eye. It was just standing there behind a fence, wearing some sort of peacoat, staring me down. I couldn't tell if he meant any harm.

At one in the morning I couldn't think of many reasons for him to be there, glaring at me. Maybe he thought I was the shadowy figure and didn't know what I was doing there? I lay down, trying to put myself back together.

I later turned over, slowly trying to focus back on what I was doing. Not much time passed before I got a stroke of panic. It was terror. I was getting all paranoid it was like a new side of me I'd never seen. I was thinking at the time, *I'm not going to let this stop me, I'm not going to let my fear make me go home.*

As I started to grow stronger in my belief and in myself I noticed that I was actually having a positive impact on those around me. My belief on a bigger scale is quite important. "Change starts with you" is a belief that people could use to change their lives along with others. This is a belief that could, and is, currently changing people's worlds. Everyone should make the change within themselves first.

Most people probably do believe this, but putting it into action is harder than it sounds.

The idea that change starts with you is a mentality. I think this mentality will take you places and, most importantly, it will open doors to new, sometimes unexpected, opportunity. I am glad that I took responsibility for my own life.

Honesty Williams is fourteen years old and was born in San Francisco. She has a three-year-old Chihuahua named Goldie. She has many best friends and likes hanging out with them in her free time. But her real love is art and drawing. Honesty plans to be an artist one day and will decorate her world with her sketches and drawings. Honesty also likes the color blue, hip-hop and R&B music, scary movies, and *The Babysitter's Club* comics. If she could have a superpower, she would fly!

LOVE IS JUST A BOX OF COOKIES

BY HONESTY WILLIAMS

While some may believe in love at first sight, I believe that love does not live—this means that it's not always what you expect. This is way different from "love never dies," which is a theme you hear in movies, books, and plays. There's a time we all have when our feelings and thoughts don't matter at all, when we're somebody else's side story and everything is just a game to that person. But what I'm about to tell you explains it all, so let me put my cards on the table and begin.

All my feelings were like cookie crumbs in a wrapper waiting to be thrown away. This is where my cookie falls apart: when I really gave my heart away and it never got put back, when I felt that I couldn't love anymore or had no love to give. I felt empty inside. Listen: my friends are like sugar cookies; my family's a big gingerbread cookie. I know there are a lot of cookies in the world, but sometimes you only want that specific one. The cookie I wanted was different.

It all started beginning my ninth-grade year at Mission High School. I never thought I'd see him at all. When we were in eighth grade we went to different schools. I started seeing him a lot in middle school when we always caught the same bus, and I got to know him very well during a thirty-minute bus ride when we talked face-to-face. I didn't expect to see him again.

At first I didn't feel anything at all. I was just like a friend to him, but from then on I didn't know what we were or what we were doing because he started to text me a lot. *What kind of cookie is this?* I wondered. It's not like the usual chocolate chip. Our friendship was getting stronger. The longer we talked the closer we got. I took a bite of my cookie, with a kiss.

Now I'm going to fill you in. Later I found out that everything I told just you was all a lie that I believed at the time. I'm not good at playing games, and I got played. You're probably thinking, "Well, what do you mean you just got played?" I mean I got played! Emotions down the drain, feelings down the drain, and my heart down the drain! I felt empty inside—ring a bell? Some of your thoughts and ideas are not always going to matter. Obviously in this situation mine were worthless and not good enough. *If you love something let it go, and if it comes back to you then it's yours*...blah, blah, yeah, yeah. I get it, but I gave my cookies away to the wrong person and I didn't have any left. But love *is* like a fairy tale, literally: sometimes it's not real. The next time I decide to catch feelings, remind me to play my cards right.

You should still take the risk and love other people, but think about it first before you get close to that person. Don't try too deeply to take the time to put your feelings out there with someone unless you think about it first and you know everything seems right. Think about whether you're ready to love a person that deeply before you give it your all. Love doesn't come easy.

The advice I would give someone else about love in general is that when you don't know what's going on, you need closure. You need closure to clear your mind from thinking about that person the way you used to.

From there, life goes on, and you live it.

HONESTY WILLIAMS

"From there, life goes on, and you live it."

ACKNOWLEDGMENTS

FROM US AT 826 VALENCIA

The Young Authors' Book Project is an annual labor of love that relies heavily on the generosity and dedication of an incredible number of people.

We'd first like to thank the community at Mission High School for being such a welcoming and inclusive collaborator for this project. We'd especially like to thank Mission High's Principal, Eric Guthertz, and the Assistant Principal, Laura Parker, for welcoming 826 Valencia and other great resources for students into their school. Thank you also to the staff, administrators, and students who make Mission High such a great place to be.

We are honored to have worked with an incredible partner teacher on this project, Max Anders. Mr. Anders is an outstanding educator in every way: he knows his students well and celebrates them as he pushes them to succeed, works tirelessly to ensure that everyone has access to the greatest support and most authentic opportunities possible, and inspires confidence and enthusiasm among all who set foot in his classroom. For these reasons and more, Mr. Anders was a dream collaborator for this project. We look forward to seeing the many ways in which his students will carry the skills and confidence they've gained in his classes with them as they move through the world.

It was a tremendous honor to share this manuscript with Glynn Washington, and we are endlessly grateful to him for being moved to write a foreword for this book. Mr. Washington's work is a great testament to the power of storytelling and the importance of amplifying voices that might otherwise go unheard, and his thoughtful participation in this project have allowed us to do just that. Thank you, Glynn, for believing not only in these young authors' abilities, but for your deep belief in the sharing of their words with a wide audience.

This project would not have been possible without an incredible cohort of volunteer tutors. These tutors spent two sometimes very early mornings a week working one-on-one with the young authors collected here as they wrote and edited their essays. The dedication, talent, and time they gave to the task was awe-inspiring and invaluable. Our deepest thanks to: Alyssa Aninag, Anna Gross, Brittani Hunter, Caroline Kangas, Carolyn Schultz Plakias, Clay Courchaine, Colton Hicks, Conan Putnam, Darryl Forman, Desta Lissanu, Don Sorsa, Eve Lebwohl, Halley Roberts, Hannah Darling, Izel Jimenez Ruiz, Jen Baxter, Jena Donlin, Jenna Jordan, Jennifer Lin, Jennifer Braun, Jessica Ramirez, Jessica Stahlke, Jonathan Forster, Kait Steele, Katrina Wagner, Katya Bitar, Kevin Wofsy, Krista Kujat, Lessley Anderson, Lindsey Bourne, Louise Shultz, Lucy Unwin, Maggie Andrews, Marcus Lund, Maren Smith, Mari Amend, Mari Gott, Melissa Van Gelder, Michelle Lee, Naveen Agrawal, Nell Waters, Pablo Baeza, Randi Murray, Roanne Lee, Ryan Haas, Shannon Lamborn, Shauna Bogetz, Sonia Hernandez, Sonja Swift, Tara Lira, Tehan Carey, Terri Cohn, William Poole, William Spongberg, and Wren Brennan.

One group of students and volunteer tutors took their dedication to this book above and beyond by coming to 826 Valencia after school to hand-edit each of the essays collected here, and to set the editorial direction for the book. The editorial board showed incredible professionalism and growth over the course of this process. In just five weeks, these students went from authors to co-editors, and in doing so they gained confidence in their writing skills and became empowered to make the big decisions that made this book a reality. Their hard work shines on these pages. As such, we'd like to extend a special thanks to Yancy Castro, Elise Wise, Henry Bradley, Alejandra Galvan, Riley Clark, Sian Laing, Christopher Archilla, Elia Gonzalez, Emajae Hackett, Kevin Wofsy, Halley Roberts, Eve Lebwohl, Darryl Forman, Shauna Bogetz, Ryan Haas, Terri Cohn, William Poole, Lindsey Bourne, Mari Amend, Jessica Ramirez, Tehan Carey, and Naveen Agrawal.

Enormous thanks to Lauren Mulkey, the designer of this book, for honoring the young authors' words by giving them such a beautiful home, and to Adam Bienvenu, for production assistance. To María Inés Montes, our Design Director, and Amy Popovich, our Production Coordinator, thank you both for amplifying the students' voices with your design expertise, and for keeping us all on deadline. Enormous thanks to Will Georgantas, our volunteer copy editor, for making sure every comma was in its proper place and letting the students' voices shine through.

We are also deeply grateful to an anonymous donor for being the primary fiscal sponsor of the 2015 Young Authors' Book Project. We are able to share these stories, which may not otherwise be heard, because of this support.

Finally, we are so proud of the young writers collected here. Writers, for sharing your unique and poignant perspectives with us, for your courage in offering your stories and voices to the world, and for never giving up on the writing process, we commend and profoundly thank you.

Molly Parent

PROGRAM MANAGER & EDITOR

826 VALENCIA

OUR MISSION

826 Valencia is a nonprofit organization dedicated to supporting under-resourced students ages six to eighteen with their creative and expository writing skills and to helping teachers inspire their students to write. Our services are structured around the understanding that great leaps in learning can happen with one-on-one attention and that strong writing skills are fundamental to future success.

OUR PROGRAMS

AFTER-SCHOOL TUTORING

During the school year, 826 Valencia is packed five days a week with neighborhood students who come in after school for free one-on-one tutoring in all subject areas. During the summer, these students participate in our five-week Exploring Words Summer Camp, where we explore science and creative writing through projects and writing prompts in a super-fun environment.

IN-SCHOOLS

We bring teams of volunteers into high-need schools around the city to support teachers and provide one-on-one assistance to students as they tackle various projects, including school newspapers, research papers, oral histories, and college entrance essays. We give additional support to nearby Everett Middle and Mission High schools, where we staff two dedicated 826 Writers' Rooms to support the teachers and students on site throughout the year. We also have a satellite after-school program for third, fourth, and fifth graders at Buena Vista Horace Mann, a bilingual K–8 school in the Mission District, in which English Language Learners work on creative writing to build their skills.

WORKSHOPS

826 Valencia offers free workshops designed to foster creativity and strengthen writing skills in a wide variety of areas such as cartooning, college entrance essay writing, or starting a 'zine. All workshops, from the playful to the practical, are project-based and are taught by experienced, accomplished professionals. Over the summer, our Young Authors' Workshop provides an intensive writing experience for high-school-age students over the course of two weeks.

FIELD TRIPS

Up to four times a week, 826 Valencia welcomes an entire class for a morning of wacky high-energy learning. Our most popular field trip is one in which students write their own books and take home a bound copy complete with professional illustrations, all within a two-hour period.

COLLEGE AND CAREER READINESS

Each year, we offer a roster of programs designed to help students get to college and be successful there. We provide six $15,000 scholarships to graduating seniors for their college education, serve two hundred students annually via the Great San Francisco Personal Statement Weekend (where students receive undivided attention on their college entrance essays), and partner with ScholarMatch to offer college access workshops for our seventh to twelfth graders during evening tutoring.

PUBLISHING

Students in all of 826's programs have the ability to experience, appreciate, create, and recognize great writing in part because of our professional-quality publishing. In addition to the Young Authors' Book Project, 826 Valencia publishes newspapers, books, chapbooks, and websites—all written by students. Experienced editors and designers are involved in these projects to give students greater insight into the realities of professional publishing. Our student books are publicized through our website, community events, and the local media, and some are sold nationwide.

TEACHER OF THE MONTH

From the beginning, 826 Valencia's goal has been to support teachers. There are so many students who have had their minds set aglow by a teacher's own zest for life and learning, and we'd like to play a very small part in rewarding them. Teachers are nominated by students, parents, and others who send in letters, pictures, and videos letting us know how special the teacher is. Every month we hear about so many amazing teachers, and we've been moved to tears more than once. The monthly winner receives a check for $1,500. To nominate a teacher for this award, please visit our website.

THE STAFF OF 826 VALENCIA

Bita Nazarian
Executive Director

Allyson Halpern
Development Director

Amy Popovich
Production Coordinator

Ashley Varady
Program Manager

Caroline Kangas
Pirate Store Manager

Christina V. Perry
Program Director

Claudia Sanchez
Program Coordinator

Emma Peoples
Program Assistant

Jorge Eduardo Garcia
Program Director

Lauren Hall
Director of Grants and Evaluation

María Inés Montes
Design Director

Molly Parent
Program Manager

Olivia White Lopez
Volunteer Engagement Manager

AMERICORPS SUPPORT STAFF THROUGH SUMMER 2015

Alyssa Aninag
Volunteer Engagement Associate

Amanda Loo
Development Associate

Desta Lissanu
Programs Assistant

Pablo Baeza
Programs Assistant

BOARD OF DIRECTORS

CO-FOUNDERS

We extend our deepest thanks to all of our donors, including our 2013–14 Shipmates Society leadership supporters, whose generosity makes this annual project possible.

IT'S
ALWAYS
A GOOD TIME
TO GIVE

WE NEED YOUR HELP

We could not do what we do without the thousands (yes, thousands) of volunteers who make our programs possible. It's easy to become a volunteer and a bunch of fun to actually do it. Please fill out our online application to let us know you'd like to lend your time: 826valencia.org/volunteer.

OTHER WAYS TO GIVE

Whether it's loose change or heaps of cash, a donation of any size will help 826 Valencia continue to offer a variety of free literacy and publishing programs to Bay Area youth.
We would greatly appreciate your financial support.

PLEASE MAKE A DONATION AT:

826valencia.org/donate

YOU CAN ALSO MAIL YOUR CONTRIBUTION TO:

826 Valencia Street, San Francisco, CA 94110

Your donation is tax-deductible. What a plus! Thank you!